Editing:
The Design of Rhetoric

S. Dragga and G. Gong

Baywood's Technical Communications Series
Series Editor: JAY R. GOULD

Baywood Publishing Company, Inc.
AMITYVILLE, NEW YORK

Library of Congress Catalog Number: 88-36434
ISBN: 0-89503-060-8 (cloth)
ISBN: 0-89503-059-4 (paper)

ACKNOWLEDGMENTS

Crystal, D., and D. Davy, *Investigating English Style*. Indiana University Press,
Bloomington, 1969. Adaptation of original material is by permission of
Longman Group UK Limited.

Ede, L. and A. Lunsford, Audience Addressed/Audience Invoked: The Role of
Audience in Composition Theory and Pedagogy, *College Composition and
Communication, 35*, pp. 155-171, 1984. Quotations of original material are
reprinted with permission. Copyright © 1984 National Council of Teachers
of English.

Lanham, R. A., *Revising Business Prose*, Scribner's, New York, 1981. Quotations
of original material are reprinted with permission of Macmillan Publishing
Company. Copyright © 1981 Richard A. Lanham.

Library of Congress Cataloging-in-Publication Data

Editing : the design of rhetoric / Sam Dragga and Gwendolyn Gong.
     p.   cm. - - (Baywood's technical communications series)
    Bibliography: p.
    Includes index.
    ISBN 0-89503-060-8. - - ISBN 0-89503-059-4 (pbk.)
    1. Technical editing. 2. Editing. 3. English language- - Rhetoric.
I. Dragga, Sam. II. Gong, Gwendolyn. III. Series: Baywood's
technical communications series (Unnumbered)
T11.4.E34   1989
808'.0666- -dc19   88-36434
                                                       CIP

Table of Contents

List of Tables and Illustrations

Figures   **Page**

Figures   **Page**

Figures   **Page**

Preface

Editing: The Design of Rhetoric is intended to familiarize readers with the theoretical basis and practical applications of the editing process. This involves the examination of the rhetorical canons—invention, arrangement, style, and delivery—and the corresponding rhetorical objectives of editing—accuracy, clarity, propriety, and artistry. The key objectives of this book are the following:

- to show that editing is not merely a mechanical procedure, but a complex and creative process;
- to demonstrate that the editor's job is to mediate the writer-reader relationship, and therefore requires a sensitivity to both the writer's aims and the reader's needs;
- to emphasize the importance of the rhetorical canons in the editing process by briefly explaining their historical evolution and current implications;
- to exemplify the application of rhetorical theory in the editing of three major categories of texts—technical, news, and promotional publications;
- to provide a series of heuristics for analyzing the verbal and visual characteristics of a text;
- to identify the process of editing as applicable to writers and readers in all disciplines and to the texts of all disciplines.

We envision a diverse audience for this book. For aspiring editors, we offer an introduction to rhetorical principles as a vehicle for developing a repertoire of theoretically sound and effective editing strategies. For professionals—directors of communications, public relations specialists, experienced writers and editors of professional and technical publications—this book will serve as a reference and guide, reinforcing their intuitive understanding and appreciation of the art of editing.

As both the introduction to the subject and reference source, this book covers the traditional topics associated with editing (e.g., style guides, editing symbols, typography). In addition, we introduce a variety of new ways of approaching both routine and special editorial designs. We show how a deter-

9

mination of verbal-visual orientation, an analysis of the dimensions of style, and a consideration of retinal variables and their corresponding semantic properties inform an editor's judgments regarding a text. This integration of the traditional and the innovative, we believe, is the major contribution of this book.

Our collaborative effort in writing, revising, editing, and designing this book has been a similar union of traditional and innovative processes. Often we have composed individually and edited jointly; usually, however, we have genuinely written together at the word processor, with virtually four hands touching the keys.

We gratefully acknowledge the guidance of Norman Cohen, President of Baywood Publishing Company. We also appreciate the support and encouragement we have received from the College of Liberal Arts and the Department of English, Texas A&M University.

Above all, the patience, understanding, and support of our families—Linda, Timothy, and Nicholas Dragga, and John and Devereux Powers—have been essential to both the inception and completion of this book.

CHAPTER 1

The Canons of Rhetoric

Editors are artists. And, as artists, editors must be prepared to be actively engaged in every phase of the creative process culminating in their art—the text. They may take other writers' texts and help shape them for presentation to readers, or they may compose texts themselves, using their expertise in the craft of writing; they may weave together a number of works into a tapestry— an edition or collection of texts; they may design the actual aesthetic presentation of texts—typeface, type size, paper, etc. It is this identification with the artist that yields an effective editor, for written discourse represents art—from the time it is a part of a writer's imagination to the time its shape is determined through trial and error, to the time its form becomes distinct and stylistically pleasing, to the time the work is presented for others to read. Understanding the rhetorical repertoire of editors is the purpose of this book.

The underlying premise in this book is that rhetorical theory provides the basis or philosophical foundation for the editor's judgments. As such, the rhetorical canons serve as a fitting and logical way of approaching the editing of texts. We have therefore divided the text into four major parts: *invention, arrangement, style,* and *delivery*.

Invention involves the discovery of the purpose or aim of the discourse, audience analysis, strategies for generating and gathering ideas. According to discourse theorist James L. Kinneavy, the major principle of organization for a text is its purpose or aim [1]. He describes the major aims of discourse as 1) expressive (friendly letters and essays), 2) referential (research reports and news articles), 3) persuasive (editorials and advertisements), and 4) literary (short stories, lyrics, and drama). It is necessary that writers understand the aim of their discourse in order to satisfy the informational needs and expectations of their audience.

Analysis of an audience is thus also a crucial consideration. In their research on the concept of audience, Lisa Ede and Andrea Lunsford distinguish between two perceptions of audience: *audience addressed* and *audience invoked* [2]. According to their research, "Those who envision audience as addressed emphasize the concrete reality of the writer's audience; they also share the assumption that knowledge of this audience's attitudes, beliefs, and expectations is not only possible (via observation and analysis) but essential" [2, p. 156]. In contrast to the notion of audience addressed is *audience invoked*: "the writer uses the semantic and syntactic resources of language to provide cues for the reader—cues which help to define the role or roles the writer wishes the reader to adopt in responding to the text" [2, p. 160]. To understand audience as either addressed or invoked, however, leads to oversimplification of the concept of *audience*. Writers need to know how to address a "real" audience as well as a "fictional" audience, and thus need to acknowledge both types. Without this understanding, writers will be unable to determine what information the audience needs and expects, and therefore what information to gather.

The gathering of this information for the audience involves invention strategies and researching. In their composition text, *Four Worlds of Writing* [3], Lauer, Montague, Lunsford, and Emig stress invention, emphasizing how strategies for generating information are also workable in professional writing situations. For example, they point out that brainstorming is a technique "often used in business and particularly advertising" and the journalistic formula is that which "has long been used by members of the news media" [3, pp. 511–512]. These invention strategies reveal to writers what they already know about their subjects, thus what they don't know and need to find out. It is the function of researching to fill in these gaps. Researching begins with the interviewing of those who have this information. When this use of oral sources proves either impossible or insufficient, writers turn to written sources of information.

The editor's job is to determine the accuracy of the information gathered and suggest to writers alternative sources of information, as necessary. In addition, the editor determines whether the information gathered fits the communicative aim and satisfies the information needs and expectations of the audience.

Keeping in mind the aim and audience, writers must organize their information. *Arrangement* is this organization of a text, the ordering of information according to appropriate cognitive patterns. Depending on the purpose or aim of the text, how the information is most effectively organized will differ. For example, a narrative invites readers to expect a chronological organization, while a description elicits the expectation of a spatial organization of detail. A discussion of similarities and differences or causes and effects leads readers to anticipate a climactic organization.

Editors must be adept at analyzing the clarity of a text's organization. One effective method of accomplishing this is to consider cohesion, the set of semantic resources for linking a given sentence to a previous sentence. What are some properties of discourse that are present in a cohesive text—in, for example, a paragraph? According to text linguists M. A. K. Halliday and R. Hasan, two properties that form a basic taxonomy for cohesion are *ties* and *topic-comment* [4]. A tie refers to a single instance of cohesion. More specifically, a tie signals one occurrence of a pair of semantically related items (e.g., *The tanks* contain at least 1.5 days' worth of reactant. *They* are designed to store this amount to assure continuous operation of the facility in case of a missed delivery). In addition to ties, there is also the property of *topic-comment*. Topic refers to a subject which the sentence is about (often called old or "given information"), and comment refers to the new information about the topic. Underlying this type of discourse analysis is the assumption that writers are motivated to communicate something which readers do not know or at least do not have in the focus of their attention. Editors, therefore, must alert their audience that something is to be communicated and prepare them by providing all the necessary contexts to make the transmission of information successful. The new information must be accompanied by at least some old information already known or explained to the audience (e.g., The tanks *store 1.5 days' worth of reactant. This supply* assures continuous operation of the facility in case of a missed delivery). This linguistic approach to analyzing the arrangement or structure of discourse is one way editors or writers can produce and evaluate texts. Editors must be familiar with both semantic and cognitive patterns in order to assess the clarity of the arrangement—the presentation of ideas—to the readership. And editors must also determine the appropriate ratio of verbal and visual information (i.e., words versus illustrations).

Equally important to effective communication is the consideration of style. As rhetorician Richard Lanham tells us, all writers are potential creators of "The Official Style," characterized as: "dominantly a noun style; a concept style; a style whose sentences have no design, no shape, rhythm, or emphasis; an unreadable, voiceless, impersonal style; a style built on euphemism and various kinds of poetic diction; above all, a style with a formulaic structure, 'is' plus a string of prepositional phrases before and after" [5, p. 81]. Lanham provides a good example of the official style:

Normal belief is that the preparation and submission of a proposal in response to a Request for Proposal (RFP), Request for Quotation (RFQ), or a bid in response to an Invitation for Bids (IFB) is no different than that of an unsolicited proposal for a grant from the National Science Foundation or another government agency; and that if such a proposal or bid is hand-delivered to the Office of Extramural Support on a Friday afternoon, it will get mailed the same day to reach Washington, D.C. by 4:00 p.m. of the following Monday. Having read this article, however, the reader, we hope, will agree that this is an erroneous belief which has led and, if continued to be believed, will lead to unhappy experiences for all concerned [5, p. 7].

Translated into a plain style:

> Unsolicited grant proposals differ from ones solicited by a Request for Proposal (RFP), a Request for Quotation (FRQ), or an Invitation for Bids (IFB). If you bring a solicited proposal to our offices on Friday afternoon, thinking it will be mailed that day and reach Washington by Monday at 4:00 p.m., you'll be disappointed. We hope this article has shown you why [5, p. 7].

It is the editor's job to see that ideas receive expression appropriate to their importance, complexity, urgency, aim, and audience.

"Officialese" is also common in visual presentation (i.e., writers illustrate information without considering their communicative aim or audience). While numerous elaborate visuals might be impressive, as impressive as verbal officialese, writers and editors must always judge the clarity and rhetorical efficacy of their visuals. For example, while a table is less attractive and interesting than a chart or graph, it is rhetorically more effective if the readers must recall or review specific pieces of information [6, p. 133]. If the readers must be aware only of trends or relationships, then it is the appealing chart or graph which meets the readers' information needs more quickly and more persuasively. The visual aid which is incorporated only because it is available is likely to be ineffective, that is, without rhetorical justification.

While verbal style has traditionally been recognized as a critical issue for writers and editors to address, appropriate emphasis on visual style also deserves serious attention. Editors must impress upon their writers the need for a clear, concise, and emphatic style adapted to their aim and audience, both in the verbal and visual presentation of information.

The final rhetorical principle is *delivery*, the total presentation of the text. Delivery refers to document design, the appropriate design for aim and audience. It is the equivalent of effective enunciation. For example, the use of headings and indentation, design of figures and tables, the choice of typeface and typesize, and the balancing or positioning of verbal and visual presentation on the page play a significant part in whether or not the document is effective. A well-designed report indicates a writer's respect for both the work and the audience; it also aids the reader, by making the information more inviting to read and easier to understand. Because delivery influences the reader's perception of the document, it is a vital rhetorical consideration. According to Robert Connors [7, pp. 64-65],

> In contrast to the vast literature on oral delivery generated by speech scholars, the field of composition has always dealt with written delivery in a series of terse, mechanical commandments. These are usually found on a page or

two pages of a handbook . . . but writers have tended to cling desperately to the letter of their handbook laws, never bestirring themselves to investigate whether the standard manuscript format they use is the most effective.

In the following chapters, we will consider in more detail each of these rhetorical canons—invention, arrangement, style, and delivery. This division of the fluid and flexible process of editing is admittedly a simplification. However, this artificial isolation of the four major stages in the composition of a text allows us to identify the corresponding rhetorical objectives of editing: accuracy, clarity, propriety, and artistry. Integration of the rhetorical canons in the final epilogue reveals the full complexity and creativity of the editor's job. We will illustrate the practical implications of this theory by examining three categories of texts: technical publications (e.g., research reports), news publications (e.g., house organs), and promotional publications (e.g., brochures). We believe that theory must inform practice. Without this correspondence, the editor is merely a technician, given to the blind adoption of rhetorical guidelines rather than their insightful adaptation.

This book thus introduces editors to the design of rhetoric. It is this design which gives writing memorability as well as readability; it is this design which gives resonance to writing; and it is this rhetorical design which links even the most ephemeral of written communication to the timeless tradition of human discourse.

REFERENCES

1. J. L. Kinneavy, *A Theory of Discourse*, Norton, New York, 1971.
2. L. Ede and A. Lunsford, Audience Addressed/Audience Invoked: The Role of Audience in Composition Theory and Pedagogy, *College Composition and Communication, 35*, pp. 155-171, 1984.
3. J. M. Lauer, G. Montague, A. Lunsford, and J. Emig, *Four Worlds of Writing*, 2nd edition, Harper and Row, New York, 1985.
4. M. A. K. Halliday and R. Hasan, *Cohesion in English*, Longman, London, 1976.
5. R. A. Lanham, *Revising Business Prose*, Scribner's, New York, 1981.
6. B. F. Barton and M. S. Barton, Toward a Rhetoric of Visuals for the Computer Era, *The Technical Writing Teacher, 12*, pp. 126-145, 1985.
7. R. J. Connors, *Actio*: A Rhetoric of Manuscripts, *Rhetoric Review, 2*, pp. 64-73, 1983.

CHAPTER 2

Invention

RHETORICAL THEORY OF INVENTION

Invention or "inventio" is the rhetorical art of finding effective arguments and pertinent information about a subject. Some 2400 years ago, Aristotle wrote his *Rhetoric*, one of the most influential philosophical treatises on rhetorical theory [1]. In Books One and Two of this work, Aristotle demonstrates that rhetoric was a genuine discipline that could be taught, thereby refuting Plato's notion that rhetorical skill was just a natural gift [2, p. 598]. Aristotle emphasizes that the rhetorical art of persuasion rests in the notion of *probability* rather than solely on universal truths that were rarely discoverable or verifiable. According to Aristotle, rhetoric as art centers around *belief*: rhetors base their arguments on the audience's beliefs and understanding of a subject. For Aristotle, analyzing an audience's beliefs provides speakers and writers with the highest probability of success in presenting ideas to others.

In addition to his perspective on probable arguments and audience beliefs, Aristotle gives rhetors a way of understanding arguments, grouping them into two categories: inartistic proofs and artistic proofs. Inartistic proofs are those arguments based on external evidence such as witnesses and contracts. In contrast, artistic proofs are those arguments that are based on the appeal to reason (*logos*), the appeal to emotion (*pathos*), and the appeal to good will and one's personal sensibilities (*ethos*). To discover ways to apply arguments to different subjects, rhetors utilize topics as inquiry strategies; for example, the topics assist rhetors in defining, comparing, and analyzing causes and effects.

For Aristotle, the process of invention comprises 1) constructing the best "probable" arguments by considering the three appeals and the topics, and 2) analyzing audience beliefs. As it was in Aristotle's time, invention in contemporary times is a complex activity imperative for writers and editors. For writers to produce the most effective discourse for particular audiences, they need to be fully engaged in the process of invention; in like fashion, editors who review and make suggestions to writers about their discourse must also be informed of

16

the process. Occasionally, editors may find themselves participating or reenacting invention strategies with writers in order to instruct authors or discover with authors ways to strengthen their discourse. In short, good editors are themselves good writers with a full repertoire of constructive approaches to writing, especially to invention.

In this chapter we present a constructive approach to the process of invention that editors may find useful for themselves as both writers and editors. The inventional process presented here is not intended to be interpreted as a rigid one, but instead as a flexible guide for editors. Like the composing process itself, invention is a series of recursive strategies that writers employ in shaping their ideas and crafting their prose.

The process of invention entails four major stages:

1. determining the communicative aim;
2. analyzing the audience;
3. gathering information; and
4. editing for accuracy.

Communicative Aim

The focus and shape of discourse are guided by a controlling question which motivates the writer and gives the text a *raison d'etre*. As mentioned earlier, all writing attempts to realize certain purposes. In rhetorician James L. Kinneavy's theory of discourse, these purposes can be conceptualized as "aims of discourse": *expressive, referential, persuasive*, and *literary* [3]. One way of understanding these aims is by considering the communication triangle, which represents the elements found in all written discourse: writer, audience/reader, subject, and language/form (Figure 2.1 [3, p. 61]). Each piece of written discourse has all four of these elements but emphasizes one or another, thereby creating varying aims.

Writing that emphasizes the writer has an *expressive* aim. Expressive aim discourse includes "diaries, journals, . . . some religious credos or manifestoes, myths of primitive or sophisticated societies, and value systems . . . [and] uses of language whereby an individual or group expresses its intuitions and emotional aspirations" [3, pp. 38-39]. A writer composing a personal essay for the *Chronicle of Higher Education*, narrating and interpreting that first year of teaching technical writing at a major university, writes with a primarily expressive aim. The writer's own perceptions of being in the college classroom represent a personal reality, and the purpose of the essay is to "express" that reality to readers of the *Chronicle*. Editors for this publication review this writer's essay to ensure that the discourse meets this aim—despite its obvious subjectivity.

Writing that emphasizes the subject has a *referential* aim. Referential aim discourse, often called expository writing, can be classified as informative,

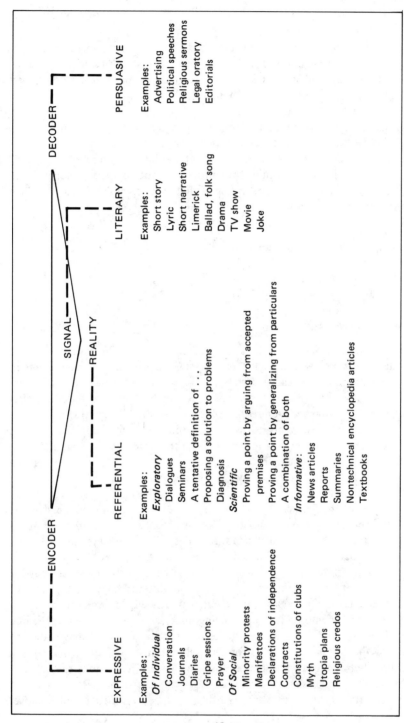

Figure 2.1. Kinneavy's "aims of discourse."

exploratory, or scientific. Examples of informative uses of language include press releases, reports, summaries, and textbooks. Scientific uses of language involve proving a point by arguing from accepted premises or proving a point by generalizing from particulars. Questionnaires, tentative definitions, and proposals offering solutions to problems are examples of exploratory uses of language.

Writing that emphasizes the audience has a *persuasive* aim. Granted, all discourse can be seen as persuasive to some degree; however, if the text focuses primarily on the audience/reader, it can be considered primarily persuasive discourse. Examples of persuasive aim discourse are advertisements, political messages, religious sermons, and editorials. All of these texts act as means to convince an audience to take action on an issue or to understand an issue.

For a hostile audience, persuasion may actually convert readers to a different opinion on a subject; for a neutral audience, persuasion may offer readers perspective and point of view on a subject; and for a friendly audience, persuasion may simply confirm or strengthen readers' convictions and beliefs about an issue. For example, a Democratic presidential nominee may write an open letter to persuade voters that she is the most able and deserving individual for the job. This letter may attempt to sway liberal Republicans to vote Democratic, to convince Independents to consider the candidate a better choice than the Republican nominee, and to reaffirm Democratics' confidence in their party's representative. In that the audience—complex as it may be—is the primary focus of the writer, the message constitutes persuasive aim discourse.

Discourse which focuses on language/form has a *literary* aim. Short stories, poetry, drama, jokes and limericks, and novels are representative of this type of written communication. While many consider all literary discourse to be literature, we make a key distinction: All written discourse—regardless of aim—is literature: that is, researchers and writers may review the literature in their field of study, be it in the humanities, the sciences, or engineering. Literature is not restricted to poetic forms alone. Discourse with a *literary* aim discourse, however, is. The writer of this literary discourse strives above all else to perfect the form language takes, to create a delicate balance of the aesthetic and semantic power of language. For example, the poet who composes an Elizabethan sonnet is guided during the composing process by the sonnet form: three quatrains and a couplet. Similarly, the joke teller is guided by the form of a joke: description of the scene (context), the narrative or dialogue, the concluding punchline.

To summarize, aims guide discourse. The basic aims of discourse are expressive, referential, persuasive, and literary. But these aims may overlap. For instance, an expressive narrative on a writer's first visit to the Grand Canyon may also be instructive, thereby referential, for readers who have never travelled there before but who are considering vacationing there next summer. A persuasive essay on drinking and driving may be framed around a writer's personal loss, resulting in a persuasive/expressive discourse. Even when aims do overlap, however, one aim will emerge as primary, and the editor as well as the writer must be able to discern this complexity in the discourse.

Audience Analysis

Aristotle initially identified audience analysis as a critical step in the invention stage of composing and defined it as a pragmatic exercise in which speakers consider the demographic variables which might determine the effectiveness of their rhetoric (e.g., age, education). The modern ability to gather seemingly infinite amounts of demographic information on audiences, however, requires that the gathering of data be limited to only that information which has relevance to the speaker's specific communicative aim. This purpose-oriented analysis is the initial modification of the Aristotelian formulation: instead of asking all possible questions about a particular audience, the speaker asks only those questions that deal with the rhetor's specific rhetorical purpose. "The search for information is then governed by what it is that the speaker needs to know about his audience in the context of a given communication situation" [4, pp. 44-45].

While Aristotle's formulation influences subsequent theory and research on audience analysis, it is especially his emphasis on oral communication and therefore on stereotypes of homogeneous social groupings which proves problematic in the adaptation of audience analysis to the written medium. Some additional modification is necessary because of the intrinsic differences between speaker-listener and writer-reader relationships.

Spoken language is localized within time and space and, unless it is electronically recorded, linked to the single situation within which it occurs. Speakers and their listeners are engaged in a social situation and thus are subject to the nervousness, tension, joy, exhilaration of being in a social situation, are faced with common distractions (e.g., sights, sounds, smells), and are bound by the appropriate cultural patterns of social behavior. In addition, the speaker, composing in front of the audience, has the opportunity to be receptive to and intimate with a known, specific individual or a known, specific, and typically homogeneous grouping of individuals: that is, speakers and listeners usually have a common bond which brings them together for the social experience of speaking and listening, be it the bond of friendship, family, religion, occupation, etc. The speaker also has the opportunity to assess continuously what is being said and how it is being said in accordance with the visible or vocal guidance of the listener or listeners [5, pp. 277-279].

Written language, however, typically communicates across time and space. The writer, while composing, is always isolated, without the guidance of the reader or readers: thus the writer is never entirely certain that the intended message is being clearly communicated. Similarly unclear to the writer is the precise readership of the message (e.g., a memo written to a subordinate might be shown to a superior, or a research proposal designed for internal circulation only might be accidently or intentionally distributed externally). And equally obscure is how the message is received—with mild praise, wild delight, thorough disinterest, stinging ridicule, impassioned denunciation [5, pp. 281-282].

Because speakers communicate to a visible and/or vocal audience and writers to invisible and silent readers, the energy given the differing communication processes differs also:

> In a speech situation, the speaker has ways of encouraging or pressing for more energy than the listener might initially want to give. He can, for example, use attention-getting gestures or grimaces, or he can play upon the social responsiveness of his listener; the listener, in turn, can query or quiz or withhold his nods until he has received the "goods" he requires from the speaker.
>
> Nothing like this open bargaining can go on in the writing situation, where the writer cannot keep an eye on his reader nor depend upon anything except words on a page to get him his due of attention [6, pp. 11-12].

The separation of writer and reader in time and space, however, also yields distinct advantages for written communication. Though the speaker can solicit efforts at understanding from an audience, listeners usually depend entirely on the speaker to communicate the message clearly and believe little or no expense of energy ought to be required of them. Readers, however, are usually less languid, expecting to exert themselves in order to comprehend the writer's message [7, p. 10].

In addition, because spoken language is perceived as it is being vocalized, the rate of communication, words per unit of time, is set for the receiver by the transmitter, who chooses to speak quickly or slowly as necessary; the listener has to keep pace with the speaker or signal the speaker that the pace is inappropriate. Because writing always occurs prior to reading, it is ultimately the receiver who determines the rate of communication [8, p. 45].

Time therefore imposes serious limitations on the speaker and listener, limitations which the writer and reader essentially escape:

> The writer can makes notes, write sections as they become clear, uniting them later, ponder difficult problems as long as need be. The reader in turn can read at his own speed, refer back to what he has read earlier, read the last chapter first, skip uninteresting sections and ponder over profound formulations and obscurities. . . .
>
> In speech much of this freedom does not exist. The unfolding of the utterance in time is inexorable and speaker and listener alike are bound

together in the same situation to the same one-dimensional, one-directional flow of talk [9, p. 68].

But what does this mean for audience analysis? It means that the kind of audience the speaker addresses is significantly different from the kind of "audience" a writer addresses. The writer addresses an invisible reader or group of readers or groups of readers. The writer's audience is of uncertain, possibly unlimited, and probably heterogeneous composition. Audience response to the writer is either nonexistent or delayed, and it is the readers who decide how quickly or slowly to receive the writer's message, which passages of the message to ignore and which to scrutinize, which to skim and which to review. This means that audience analysis as Aristotle identifies and defines it is a less than satisfactory model for written communication.

Several modifications or expansions of the Aristotelian model are therefore necessary. The first of these deals with the uncertainty and heterogeneity of the audiences. While Aristotle describes the analysis of a known specific audience, the writer has no similar acquaintance with the composition and limits of the audience. Thus it is important for the writer to identify the primary audience and the secondary audience or audiences for a particular document [10, pp. 21-22]. That is, besides the individual or individuals being addressed, writers must also consider additional or subsequent readers of the document.

With this recognition of multiple audiences for a written document comes the awareness of the differing informational needs and motivations of those audiences [11, pp. 131-132]. Different audiences will be more or less familiar with the subject, more or less positively disposed toward the subject, more or less educated, more or less professionally or technically experienced.

The second modification of the Aristotelian model deals with the rate and sequence of the audience's reception of the text. The multiple audiences of a document will have different information needs, and the urgency with which those audiences will read a given text will vary. It is thus crucial for the writer to determine how quickly or slowly the audience will need to read a given document and to aid the audience's reading by the inclusion or exclusion of information, by the choice of visual and/or verbal presentation of that information, by the clear identification of information blocks, etc.

The third modification involves the reader's environment. Because written language communicates across time and space, it is necessary for the writer to consider the physical and temporal environment of his or her readers, that is, the interruptions and distractions which the reader might be subject to, the various circumstances which might interfere with the reader's reception of the writer's message.

It is this modified and modernized Aristotelian formulation of audience analysis which Lisa Ede and Andrea Lunsford describe as audience addressed

[12]. A pragmatic, purpose-oriented conception of audience, it typically comprises a series of questions which the writer attempts to answer based on observations and assumptions about that audience (e.g. [13, pp. 43-44]). But this procedure, as well as the entire notion of addressing the audience, has been criticized as subject to superficial and simplistic distortion primarily because it is impossible for the writer to know his or her audience in the way that a speaker does. Walter J. Ong, for example, argues that writers must create their audience, assigning the readers of a text a fictional role to play while reading the discourse; the readers in turn must accept their assigned role [14, p. 12]. Thus both writer and reader cooperate in a fictitious relationship established by a series of informational signals given by the writer and received by the reader. It is this conception of audience that Ede and Lunsford identify as audience invoked [12].

Neither of these conceptions of audience by itself, however, entirely circumscribes the writer-reader relationship. Ede and Lunsford thus offer a synthesis of these two perspectives:

> The addressed audience, the actual or intended readers of a discourse, exists outside of the text. Writers may analyze these readers' needs, anticipate their biases, even defer to their wishes. But it is only through the text, through language, that writers embody or give life to their conception of the reader. In so doing, they do not so much create a role for the reader . . . as invoke it. Rather than relying on incantations, however, writers conjure their vision—a vision which they hope readers will actively come to share as they read the text—by using all the resources of language available to them to establish a broad, and ideally coherent, range of cues for the reader [12, p. 167].

If, for example, in a publication on driving drunk, the writer wishes readers to consider the ethical implications of drinking and driving, it will be necessary for the writer to invoke for the readers the role of a fair-minded, morally sensitive individual. The writer does this by providing information signals to the readers that this is the role they are to engage in while reading this document. These signals can be either visual or verbal: prose narratives describing the innocent victims of drunk drivers or photographs of the innocent victims. However, it is also necessary for the writer to consider the audience addressed, for there will be some readers who will be more likely to accept the invoked role of a morally sensitive individual—namely, those who do not drink and drive; and there will be some readers who will be more likely to reject this role—namely, those who do drink and drive. For the latter, a more effective invocation might be to the role of law abiding citizen or self-interested individual, with visual and verbal information signals emphasizing the physical and legal risks and consequences of drunk driving.

This synthesis of audience addressed and audience invoked also has bearing on the communicative aim. If, for example, the writer wishes to stop people from drinking and driving, then the invocation of the role of morally sensitive individual is inappropriate, as analysis of the addressed audience likely to accept this invocation reveals: those most likely to accept this role are those who do not drink and drive. (If the writer's aim is to encourage nondrinking drivers to act against drinking drivers, then this is the appropriate role to invoke.) But if the writer's aim really is to stop people from driving drunk, then the invocation of the law abiding citizen or self-interested individual is more likely to be accepted by the addressed audience of drunk drivers. Thus the writer's relationship with the readership, the audience addressed and the audience invoked, has a significant effect on the communicative aim as well as on the kinds of information, both verbal and visual, which the writer must give the readers.

Information Gathering

In addition to considering communicative aim and audience, writers need to turn their attention to the task of gathering information. This stage consists of two major inquiry phases: *internal dialogue* and *external dialogue*.

The most natural and yet most important starting point for this task is a writer's own knowledge about a subject. For this reason, internal dialogue is crucial in this stage. By internal dialogue, we mean that writers carry out "conversations" with themselves to determine and therefore inventory what is known about the topic.

Internal Dialogue

Writers typically find the task of writing easier and more meaningful if they have some personal involvement in what they are trying to write about. To determine what self-knowledge or personal experience, if any, they have about their subject, they can employ a variety of strategies for starting an internal dialogue. In this section, we present five possible approaches to discovery: brainstorming, inner dialogue, pentad, notational and graphic techniques, and Aristotelian invention. Some writers experiment with these strategies to learn which ones work best for different types of writing and aims of discourse. For example, marketing executives report that brainstorming is one of the most effective means for them to discover novel ideas or "angles" of advertising a new product. Engineers, on the other hand, often prefer graphic techniques of invention as a means to visualize their subject. Still other writers swear by a combination of techniques, insisting that they can come to understand their subject's complexity more effectively if they use Aristotelian invention as well as brainstorming or graphic techniques.

When working with authors, editors need to understand what writers have written, and, if any information appears to be ambiguous or incomplete, editors are obliged to help them locate such weaknesses for revision. One of the most effective ways for editors to assist writers at this stage is to identify which techniques the writers have used and then review the information-gathering processes with them. As a result, editors must be familiar with internal dialogue techniques.

Brainstorming

This technique requires writers to jot down personal knowledge about the subject. Writers need not worry about the order or logic of the ideas, but instead simply relax and inventory all related thoughts that come to mind about the writing topic.

Inner Dialogue

This type of internal dialogue represents an involuntary method of inquiry. Inner dialogue is similar to writers conducting formal interviews or conversations with themselves. Inner dialogue, or thinking aloud, is a natural phenomenon, for when confronted with a task or a problem, writers will naturally begin to internalize the rhetorical situation, which in turn will lead to an inner dialogue directed toward problem solving. For many writers, this technique is brainstorming aloud: instead of writing down associated ideas, they tape record their inner dialogue or reconstruct their dialogue in writing at a later time. Because formulating ideas and speaking come so naturally and involuntarily, the act of dialogue is typically quite effective for most writers.

Pentad

A rhetorical contribution of rhetorician Kenneth Burke, the pentad consists of five topics: act (what was done?), scene (when or where was it done?), agent (who did it?), agency (how did he or she do it?), and purpose (why did he or she do it?) [15, pp. 155-156]. Pairing the topics or creating ratios yields investigative power. For example, a ratio of act/scene focuses on the reason a particular event occurred in a particular place. Burke's pentad is often associated with the journalist's key questions: who? what? when? where? why? how? The pentad provides writers with an effective and efficient means of discovering information.

Notation and Graphic Techniques

This strategy involves the visual representation of ideas. Writers obviously do this when committing ideas to paper; however, this strategy also requires that other visual displays of information be made to show various relationships among ideas. For example, writers may draw flow charts to identify stages in a process, tree diagrams to see hierarchical relationships, bar graphs to reveal similarities or differences, and brackets, arrows, or boxes to determine causes and effects. It is customary to present important and oftentimes complicated information in the form of visual aids, but this type of visual representation may also be used to help writers realize the logical shape the discourse is taking. Rather than relying on memory to aid in sorting and organizing information, writers discover order while uncovering the construct of that information.

Aristotelian Invention

Aristotelian invention has as its basis the classical notion of topoi or topics: the various locations in the rhetor's mind of information about a subject:

Definition
  A. Genus
  B. Division

Comparison
  A. Similarity
  B. Difference
  C. Degree

Relationship
  A. Cause and Effect
  B. Antecedent and Consequence
  C. Contraries
  D. Contradictions

Circumstance
  A. Possible and Impossible
  B. Past Fact and Future Fact

Testimony
  A. Authority
  B. Testimonial
  C. Statistics
  D. Maxims
  E. Law
  F. Precedents (Examples)

This type of heuristic can guide a writer through a systematic inquiry so that an inventory of all possible information available either for supporting propositions or for testing and modifying them can be made.

External Dialogue

After discovering through internal dialogue their own knowledge about a subject, writers begin to consult outside sources for additional information. This stage in the inquiry process is external dialogue. There are two types of external dialogue that may be pertinent and necessary when gathering information.

Interviewing Sources

By talking with authorities in a given subject area, a writer can oftentimes obtain an expeditious and clearer perspective on a topic, communicative aim, and intended audience. Those people who have academic training or personal experience in a research field can provide a writer with ways of understanding the subject, offering references to additional sources, both oral and written.

There are distinct advantages to interviewing sources:

1) *Immediacy*: Writers might get the most current answer to a question by talking to specialists in the appropriate discipline—professionals doing research on the issue. Ordinarily, a minimum of nine months elapses between the time a manuscript is written, submitted to a journal, reviewed, and either rejected or accepted for publication. If the written source is a book, the typical delay between the composing of the manuscript and the publishing of the book is at least a full year. Thus written sources never give the current information which oral sources might.

2) *Credibility*: Oftentimes, writers know their oral sources of information, the position they hold, their reputations, their credentials, their accomplishments. This allows the evaluation of the credibility of the oral sources and their responses to questions. A similar evaluation of written sources might be impractical or impossible. The writer might know who the authors of a book are, but might not know anything else about the authors (e.g., what else they might have written, what academic degree they hold, how they are regarded in their discipline).

3) *Efficiency*: Writers can ask oral sources specific questions and receive specific answers, thus saving time. During an interview, it can quickly be determined if a source has the desired information. With a written source, this is obviously impossible: writers have to examine the table of contents or the major headings, have to check the index (if available), and might have to read through substantial material before finding or failing to find pertinent information.

While speaking to sources is a good starting point in the process of external dialogue, it is rarely a satisfactory ending point. There are distinct disadvantages to using only oral sources.

1) *Inefficiency*: Because the information writers receive is being communicated orally, the ability to absorb, organize, and evaluate the information may be limited. Note-taking will be necessary, and this could jeopardize clarity and accuracy. Similarly, the specialist might be less effective in providing information on a subject orally: because the interviewer guides the direction of the discussion—the less informed participant in the dialogue—there is a risk that important ideas or connections between ideas might be omitted or distorted. For example, the interviewer might ask questions which the specialist considers illogical, irrelevant, naive, or hostile: the specialist's oral presentation of information, as a consequence, might seem disjointed and incoherent to the interviewer.

2) *Subjectivity*: A given writer's reaction to the information received is likely to be colored by prior knowledge of the person being interviewed. This personal knowledge may interfere with the writer's ability to judge objectively the information received. Written sources, however, bring a special objectivity to information. By separating the knower from that which is known, writing allows a researcher to evaluate information without the interference of personal bias. A researcher can read a book and acquire information from that book without knowing anything at all about the author.

3) *Unreliability*: The spoken word often does not carry the authority that the written word does. Articles in journals have been reviewed and judged meritorious by the editors. Similarly, books undergo a careful screening process. But what a specialist tells a writer during an interview is not always subject to review, and therefore this information is not always as reliable as written sources.

Reading Sources

At this point, therefore, a brief consideration of *reading sources* is necessary. While it may seem odd to refer to reading sources as external dialogue, that is, in fact, what the interaction between a reader and a text is. A scholar or researcher is informing the reader of research findings through writing, and the reader is processing and perhaps even questioning that information while reading.

The most important place to locate and retrieve valuable written sources is the library. By using various indexes and computer data bases of a library, a writer has access to books, journals, newspapers, government documents, films, and maps. Library research enables a writer to carry on external dialogues with written texts, and these dialogues can further the writer's understanding of or even prompt some revision of earlier conclusions.

Reading sources may require a writer to interview sources again. For example, the writer might uncover contradictory information or might desire clarification of difficult readings. Similarly, external dialogue might lead to further internal dialogue (e.g., additional brainstorming to obtain a different perspective on the topic). The process of inquiry is recursive.

Editing for Accuracy

Editing for accuracy involves determining the correctness and appropriateness of the writer's communicative aim, analysis of audience, and collected information.

Communicative Aim

Initially, the editor has to determine what the writer perceives as the communicative aim and if this is consistent with the editor's perception of a desirable or appropriate aim. For example, a journal editor desires a referential piece on the consequences of tax reform legislation, but the writer submits a persuasive piece criticizing this legislation. The editor must realize this conflict of aim and either resolve the problem or return the piece to the writer with suggestions for revision.

If the communicative aim is appropriate, the editor must then assess its clarity, determining if the purpose of the piece is explicitly or implicitly given in the text. If the communicative aim is likely to be misunderstood by readers, the editor must offer the writer strategies for identifying and clarifying the aim.

If the communicative aim is clear, the editor must determine what, if any, subordinate aims occur and if these are appropriate to the text. For example, in a referential piece on tax reform legislation, the writer might wish to demonstrate technical proficiency with the subject in order to impress superiors and thereby receive more assignments on this and related subjects. In satisfying this subordinate aim, the writer might introduce substantial technical terminology in order to demonstrate familiarity with the topic. Recognizing the writer's subordinate aim allows the editor to mediate the writer-reader relationship more effectively, maintaining a sympathetic understanding of both the needs of the writer and the needs of the reader. The editor might, therefore, while commending the writer's knowledge of the subject and possibly assuring the writer of subsequent assignments, also ask the writer to eliminate those technical terms likely to bewilder a less knowledgeable, less experienced reader.

The editor might also determine the urgency of the communicative aim. Is, for example, tax reform legislation being explained because citizens will vote on it in tomorrow's election? In next month's election? In next year's election? Is tax reform being denounced in a persuasive piece because legislators are beginning to consider it? Are about to vote for or against it? Have just voted for or against it? The urgency of the communication guides the writer and the editor in determining the appropriate information to gather for the audience as well as the appropriate perception of that audience.

Audience Analysis

The editor must next determine who the writer perceives to be the primary audience and if this is consistent with the editor's perception. For example, in composing a referential text on computer graphics for publication in a professional computer science journal, the writer most likely will be addressing computer scientists, not a general audience.

In addition, the editor must determine who the writer perceives to be the secondary audience or audiences and if this is consistent with the editor's perception. If the writer believes a referential piece on computer graphics will be read by technical writers as well as computer scientists, the writer might attempt to accommodate this secondary audience by providing a glossary of technical terminology, abbreviations, and acronyms. If the editor disagrees with the writer's perception, believing the only likely secondary audience is computer science students, the editor might omit this glossary and ask the writer for a list of references to additional sources of information on computer graphics.

If the primary and secondary audiences are appropriately perceived, the editor must determine the accuracy with which the writer has addressed the audiences, that is, the accuracy of the writer's audience analysis according to seven criteria:

1. *Education*: What is the audience's education? How extensive is their education: high school, college, advanced degrees? Is their education broad-based or specialized? What is their major field of study? Is their emphasis theoretical or technical?
2. *Professional experience*: What is the audience's professional experience? How extensive is their experience? Is their experience managerial or technical? With what kind of organization? Business? Industrial? Academic?
3. *Familiarity with subject*: How familiar is the audience with this subject? Is sufficient context supplied for both present and future readings? Is the audience likely to be bored with the subject? Is the audience likely to consider the topic their territory and thus be hostile to this discussion of the topic?
4. *Expectations*: What does the audience expect to obtain from reading this document? New information? Instructions? Recommendations? What use will the audience make of this document? Does this document fulfill the audience's expectations?
5. *Enthusiasm*: How enthusiastic is the audience about this subject? Is the audience likely to be interested in this topic? Why? Is the audience likely to be interested in this discussion of the topic? Why?

6. *Urgency*: How pressing is the audience's need to read this document? How quickly do they need to read it? How timely is the information it contains?
7. *Environment*: What is the audience's reading environment? Is there noise? Distractions? Continuous interruptions?

The editor must also determine the appropriateness of the writer's invoked audience: that is, the accuracy and sufficiency of signals indicating the relationship with the text which the writer intends the reader to have. Considering the audience addressed, the editor must judge if the invoked relationship is fitting. If it is inappropriate, the editor must offer the writer a more suitable relationship to establish between reader and text. The editor must also decide if the relationship is likely to be accepted or rejected by the addressed audience. If it is likely to be rejected, the editor must suggest strategies to the writer which will insure the audience's acceptance of the intended relationship with the text.

Gathering Information

At this point, the editor's job is to examine the appropriateness, sufficiency, reliability, plausibility, and consistency of the information. The initial consideration is how appropriate the information is, given the writer's aim and audiences. For example, in order to persuade heart surgeons that implanting mechanical hearts is a satisfactory alternative to transplanting human hearts, the writer might collect detailed medical findings comparing and contrasting the two surgical procedures, relying almost exclusively on research results and the testimony of those surgeons who have performed one or both kinds of surgery. To explain these surgical procedures to a general audience, the writer might gather instead the testimony of doctors, nurses, and patients, avoiding technical terms and explicit details.

Similarly, the editor must determine if the writer has gathered sufficient information for the aim and audience. Heart surgeons might require more details than a hospital administrator or insurance carrier. Persuading a general audience of the desirability of mechanical heart implantation might require information in addition to that necessary to explain the actual surgical procedure.

Another consideration of the editor is the reliability of information sources. The editor must assess the professional reputations of the specialists interviewed and of the books and journals researched. How recent are these sources? How often have they been cited in the field? What is the viewpoint or bias of the sources cited?

Judging the plausibility of the information is also the editor's responsibility. Deciding which information a reader might consider dubious, the editor determines its accuracy and reinforces its credibility with a citation of sources or additional explanation.

Finally, the editor must determine if the information is consistent. For example, if the writer describes the mechanical heart as 5 inches X 4 inches X 3 inches, then subsequent references in the text to the heart's size must agree with this description. Or, a patient who enters the hospital on Monday the 15th cannot have surgery on Wednesday the 18th! Nothing bewilders an audience like inconsistency, for the reader is left in a position of not knowing whether to accept the first date, the second date, or because credibility has been damaged, neither date. The editor must examine the text carefully for contradictory descriptions, events, dates, numbers, etc.

Understanding the theory of invention provides the editor with crucial insight into the composing process of the writer. Essentially, the editor is judging the accuracy with which the writer has determined the communicative aim, analyzed and invoked the audiences, and gathered information.

PRACTICE

In editing as well as in writing, theory informs and inspires practice. In this section, we will examine three major types of texts: technical publications, news publications, and promotional publications. We will present these publications, illustrating how the editor applies the theory of invention to them.

Technical publications inform or instruct readers on specialized subjects (e.g., research articles and reports, users' manuals, and proposals). News publications cover a variety of current and general topics and inform readers of coming events within their organization or community (e.g., newspapers, magazines, and house organs). Promotional publications call attention to the products or services of organizations and communities (e.g., brochures, catalogues, and business cards).

To insure the editor's thorough and logical evaluation of the writer's invention strategies, a heuristic is necessary. The following series of questions guide the editor through the major phases of the invention process and allow the editor to identify specific problems in a given text. As a heuristic, the Editor's Invention Inventory is designed to be recursive and flexible. It is not intended as a rigid and sequential description of the editing procedure (see Figure 2.2).

By referring to this inventory, the editor can then suggest solutions to problems in the text or ask the writer to address the questionable material. Typically, the editor makes these identifications and recommendations in the form of brief comments; these are usually written on small slips of paper (e.g., 3M Post-It Notes) attached to the text in appropriate places. In phrasing these comments, the editor must exercise tact and diplomacy, avoiding appropriation of the writer's text through extensive rewriting, or depreciation of the writer's text by extensive negative criticism. Questioning the author is an effective and judicious manner of calling the writer's attention to problematic passages, and these comments are commonly called *author queries*.

Communicative Aim
1. What does the writer perceive to be the communicative aim? Is it Expressive? Referential? Persuasive? Literary? 2. Is the communicative aim clearly identified or explained in the text? 3. Are there subordinate aims in the text? If so, what are they? Are they appropriate for this text?
Audience

1. Who does the writer perceive to be the primary audience for this text?
2. Who does the writer perceive to be the secondary audience for this text?
3. Has the writer appropriately analyzed the primary and secondary audiences according to
   ● Level of education?
   ● Professional experience?
   ● Familiarity with subject?
   ● Expectations?
   ● Enthusiasm?
   ● Urgency?
   ● Environment?
4. Has the writer invoked the appropriate audience?

Information Gathering
1. Has the writer gathered appropriate information? 2. Has the writer gathered sufficient information? 3. Are the information sources reliable? 4. Is the information plausible? 5. Is the information consistent?

Figure 2.2. Editor's invention inventory.

Using the following sample publications, we will illustrate how the application of the Editor's Invention Inventory yields appropriate author queries.

A Technical Publication

This sample of a technical publication is an excerpt from a research report intended for publication in a professional journal (see Figure 2.3).

Evaluation   page 15

RESULTS AND DISCUSSION

Author:
I know that you told the number of students in each group in the earlier METHODS section. Should you repeat that info here?

Curiously, students in both the control and the experimental groups showed significant increases on the Daly-Miller Writing Apprehension Test (1975) across the semester (t=-2.21, t=-2.16, p<.05). The small but signifcant increases in apprehension were clearly not expected, and, perhaps equally important, did not distinguish between the control and experimental group.

Author:
Should you give the means for the pretest and posttest of the Daly-Miller?

To test for the possibility that the Daly-Miller, as a whole, was not sensitive enough to pick up differences in students' attitudes toward evaluation of their writing, a subscale of ten items was created from that test. These ten items all probe students' attitudes about having others read their writing and about having their essays evaluated.

Author:
Should you identify here which ten items compose the subscale?

Two interesting questions emerge by considering the subscale results where students' overall apprehension increased but their apprehension about evaluation decreased: Is writing apprehension a single monolithic entity that the Daly-Miller assumes it is? And how sensitive is this test as an indicator of apprehension?

While the control group did not show significant decreases on these ten items, the experimental group improved significantly (t=2.68, p<.01). Student writers in the experimental group liked positively the one-to-one conferences in which they discussed their writing and suggestions for guided revision with their instructors. Student writers became more comfortable and confident about the evaluation process in the experimental group when their essays were rated the same by two outside readers. The rater agreement and guidelines for revision seemed to put these student writers at more ease about writing for other readers and turning in essays for evaluation.

Author:
Can you also provide the statistics for the control group?

Control group essays were graded in the traditional manner; experimental group essays were simultaneously evaluated holistically. These two different procedures were used for determining writing quality in the

Figure 2.3. Editing a technical publication for accuracy.

Evaluation   page 16

in the two groups. This difference in grading coupled
with the fact that different topics for the expressive,
referential, and persuasive essays were used to measure
pre- and post-course writing quality make it impossible
to compare the two groups directly. Improvement over
the semester can be at least estimated by comparing
grades on an early and later paper for the control
group and by comparing holistic scores of an early and
a later paper for the experimental group, nevertheless.

In the first case, the results seemed valid in
light of the fact that the instructors' grades were
purely dependent on the perceived quality of the writing (that is, not influenced by pedagogical considerations) and the writing tasks chosen from the beginning
and end of the semester made roughly the same demands
on the student writers. In the second case, the results seemed valid in light of the fact that the raters
evaluated the pre- and post-essays on the same scale
and the writing tasks were equivalent. Given the results' validity, the data suggest that both groups
improved significantly in writing quality over the
semester.

The control group showed some increase in writing
quality from the expressive essay to the persuasive
essay. However, the experimental group made
extraordinary progress from essay 1 to essay 5 (t=-
3.01, p<.01). Again, while the grades of students
whose work had been evaluated traditionally steadily
increased, their progress was not near the increase in
quality that students whose writing had been evaluated
both by summative and formative techniques. The guided
revision and one-to-one conferencing seemed to significantly increase the writing abilities of students.

To measure the reliability of raters of the experimental group's essays, a Spearman's Rho was used.
The correlation coefficients for each of the five essays were determined (#1=.39; #2=.54; #3=.74; #4=.67;
#5=.58) and averaged. The average of the coefficients
is .58, a fair correlation.

Author:

*Can you also
provide
statistics on the
control group?*

Author:

*Will your readers
know what a
Spearman's Rho
is? Or should you
briefly define it?*

Author:

*Should you
explain why .58
is considered a
fair correlation?*

Figure 2.3.   Editing a technical publication for accuracy (cont'd.)

Communicative Aim

1. *What does the writer perceive to be the communicative aim?*
   The writer perceives the communicative aim of this text as primarily referential (especially the excerpt given here). The focus is on the reporting of research findings.
2. *Is the communicative aim clearly identified or explained in the text?*
   The communicative aim of the text is clearly identified by its heading: the writer promises a straightforward presentation and explanation of the data.
3. *Are there subordinate aims in the text? If so, what are they? Are they appropriate for this text?*
   A subordinate aim of the text is to persuade readers of the authority of the writer and the significance of the research findings: the writer demonstrates familiarity with standard experimental measures and terminology (e.g., Daly-Miller Writing Apprehension Test) and uses tests of statistical significance to establish the reliability of the data. This aim is typical for a research report and is therefore appropriate for this text.

Audience

1. *Who does the writer perceive to be the primary audience for this text?*
   The writer perceives the primary audience for this text to be other researchers in the field of rhetoric and composition. Evidence of this conception of audience is the writer's focus on the validity of the writing apprehension measure.
2. *Who does the writer perceived to be the secondary audience for this text?*
   The writer perceives the secondary audience for this text as writing teachers and students. This is a study of the effects of different methods of evaluation on the attitudes of students toward writing as well as on the quality of their writing.
3. *Has the writer appropriately analyzed the primary and secondary audiences?*
   The writer has committed a common error. In satisfying the primary audience, the writer has ignored important differences between the primary and secondary audience, especially regarding their level of education, professional experience, and familiarity with the subject. Statistical evidence is typically given parenthetically with sufficient verbal explanation to satisfy the secondary audience; in the final paragraph of the excerpt, however, the discussion of the statistical information is abbreviated and thus incomprehensible without prior understanding of the subject.
4. *Has the writer invoked the appropriate audience?*
   The writer has asked the audience to perceive themselves as serious investigators of writing and the teaching of writing.

Information Gathering

1. *Has the writer gathered appropriate information?*
Information is appropriate: the focus of the discussion is the research findings. A possible exception is the third paragraph: the writer seems to be speculating on the validity of the Daly-Miller Writing Apprehension Test, instead of reporting the results of the study. Because the questions are pertinent to the data, however, this paragraph is probably within the bounds of a discussion of research results.
2. *Has the writer gathered sufficient information?*
Information is insufficient in the following cases:
a) In paragraph #1, the writer has omitted the mention of the number of students in the control and experimental group. This is covered earlier, but probably deserves repetition here for those readers who might skip over the section on methodology. The writer should also include the means for the pretest and posttest scores: this is standard practice.
b) In paragraph #2, the writer refers to a subscale of the Daly-Miller Writing Apprehension Test. Though covered earlier, this information probably deserves repetition here, possibly parenthetically.
c) In paragraph #4, the writer fails to provide data for the control group, making comparison with the experimental group impossible. The writer seems to lose objectivity and therefore credibility.
d) In paragraph #7, the writer again neglects the control group. Statistics for both the experimental and control groups are necessary if the reader is to understand and trust the research results.
3. *Are the information sources reliable?*
The Daly-Miller Writing Apprehension Test is a commonly used experimental measure. The citation of it is accurate.
4. *Is the information plausible?*
Information seems plausible. The writer's discussion of the data is unexaggerated and often qualified (e.g., "small but significant increase" or "showed some increase"). It is, however, difficult to judge plausibility without seeing the statistics for the control group: this information will indicate if the writer's claims regarding the data are justified.
5. *Is the information consistent?*
No contradictory information is evident.

A News Publication

This sample is a brief article from the newsletter of a professional association (see Figure 2.4).

Author:
Should you also give some background info as a context for this change: e.g., the system the journal is converting from or how this change will be paid for?

Author:
You use both DTP and CDP to refer to computerized desktop publishing.

Author:
Is there a way to intro this tech info more conversationally? Can you use transitions here to show that these details may interest some readers more than others?

Author:
Should you include information about other systems that are compatible?

Author:
Does your primary audience need this level of detailed explanation? Can you simplify and condense this?

[Headline]

Beginning with the Spring 1988 issue, the Texas Liberal Review (TLRev) initiates full-scale operation of a computerized desktop publishing (DTP) system to streamline editing operations and defray printing costs for the journal.

System Description

The hardware for the CDP system includes a Compaq Deskpro 286 computer (with hard drive as well as 5-1/4" floppy disk), an Apple LaserWriter Plus (with eleven resident fonts), a full-page portrait monitor, and a Microsoft serial mouse.

The software for the CDP system runs on the MS-DOS Version 3 operating system. The system uses WordPositor wordprocessing software supplemented by the PositivePublisher page layout software.

Production and Conversion Capabilities

A primary goal of the CDP system is to produce first copy and galley proofs of the TLRev issue "in house," without having to depend on (and pay for) the typesetting services of a professional printer. The edited/proofread copy is "computerized" and "output" in final form directly to a "compatible" professional print shop or printing center for high resolution production into final journal form.

A secondary goal of the CDP system is to allow scholars more participation in the typesetting of their accepted articles and reviews. For example, TLRev's new CDP system can "read" computerized versions of revised articles (processed in WordPositor on an MS-DOS system from a 5'1/4" floppy disk and mailed to the journal) with minimum document manipulation. This means, in fact, that the author "typesets" his or her own article and is, therefore, guaranteed that the version which appears in the journal is as close the the author's typographical intentions as possible.

A revised article processed in the WordPositor program (MS-DOS, 5-1/4" floppy) is the most compatible to TLRev's new CDP system, but other word processing programs are "convertible."

For example, there is a conversion program available which converts documents from WordStar or Multi-Mate (MS-DOS) to WordPositor, however, increased manipulation of the document is required as many of the "commands" (such as indentation and header/footers) of WordStar or Multi-Mate are different from those of WordPositor.

Any word processing program—for example, EasyWriter or Volkswriter—which allows a document to be converted to a "DOS file" or "ASCII file" can be read by TLRev's CDP system but, again, the document will have to be manipulated since many commands, such as underlining and superscripting, will be lost.

Figure 2.4. Editing a news publication for accuracy.

> *Author:*
> *What is the differ-*
> *ence between a*
> *"primary goal"*
> *(mentioned earlier)*
> *and a "central*
> *goal"? Is this*
> *distinction cor-*
> *rectly applied*
> *here?*
>
> Conversion is also possible for documents proc-
> essed in computer operating systems other than MS-DOS—
> for example, Apple or CDM—but the document manipulation
> is doubled as the file is converted into MS-DOS and
> then into WordPositor.
>
> Paper copy of a revised article or review is
> still welcome, of course, but there is maximum document
> manipulation involved in this "conversion" since paper
> copy must be typed into the computerized DTP system by
> a word processor operator.
>
> *Author:*
> *This is a short*
> *article, so the*
> *repetition of this*
> *information is*
> *probably unneces-*
> *sary. What do you*
> *think? Can it be*
> *cut?*
>
> Conclusion
>
> A central goal of the CDP system is to continue
> to produce the <u>Texas Liberal Review</u> in its present
> high-quality form, while modernizing and making that
> production more cost effective. The conversion to a
> desktop publishing system allows expanded capabilities
> at the cost of increased responsibilities. Members of
> the TLRev editorial staff are already at work—research-
> ing and gaining hands-on experience—to make the produc-
> tion transition smooth and efficient.

Figure 2.4. Editing a news publication for accuracy (cont'd).

Communicative Aim

1. *What does the writer perceive to be the communicative aim?*

   The writer perceives the communicative aim as referential. The emphasis is on announcing to the members of the association that publication of their journal has been computerized.

2. *Is the communicative aim clearly identified or explained in the text?*

   The informative aim is identified both by the headings (e.g., System Descrip-tion) and by the inclusion of many details about the system and its operation.

3. *Are their subordinate aims in the text? If so, what are they? Are they ap-propriate for this text?*

   Though informative, the article is also persuasive. The writer wishes to convince the members of the association and especially potential authors for the journal that this new computerized publishing system is beneficial. The writer offers a description of the advantages, without a corresponding list of disadvantages, and therefore seems intent on justifying this production change for a possibly skeptical or computerphobic audience.

Audience

1. *Who does the writer perceive to be the primary audience for this text?*

   The primary audience is the members of the association and especially those interested in submitting articles for publication in the journal.

2. *Who does the writer perceive to be the secondary audience for this text?*
A secondary audience might be prospective members of the association or prospective authors for the journal who might obtain a copy of the association's newsletter.

3. *Has the writer appropriately analyzed the primary and secondary audiences?*
The writer has appropriately analyzed the primary and secondary audiences, but has probably overestimated their familiarity with the subject and possibly their enthusiasm for it. The writer is quite specific in the description of the computerized system, relying extensively on technical terminology.

4. *Has the writer invoked the appropriate influence?*
The writer is invoking an audience that is technologically sophisticated and progressive, embracing computerization or at least tolerating it. The addressed audiences, however, might hesitate to assume this identity.

Information Gathering

1. *Has the writer gathered appropriate information?*
The information in the section titled "Production and Conversion Capabilities" is inappropriate because of its technical detail. While it is important for the writer to understand the specifics in order to write the article, the general readership will find this intimidating instead of inviting. The writer seems to have assumed that the invoked audience is identical with the addressed audience.

2. *Has the writer gathered sufficient information?*
Information is sufficient, with the following exceptions:
a) In paragraph #1, the writer might provide a context for this production change: Why did it happen? How was the journal published before? Who will pay for this change? What will it cost? etc. If readers are reluctant to accept the change to a computerized system, background information such as this might make them more receptive. The fact that such obvious questions are not addressed could leave readers both suspicious and apprehensive.
b) In paragraph #5, the writer identifies a single word processing system for the preparation of typescripts. This will give readers the impression that no other system is compatible. Is this correct? It might also imply the association's endorsement of one brand of software.
c) The final paragraph is repetitious, offering no new information.

3. *Are the information sources reliable?*
No sources of information are cited.

4. *Is the information plausible?*
The information seems plausible. More and more journals are adopting computerized publishing systems and for precisely the reasons outlined in this article.

5. *Is the information consistent?*
Two inconsistencies occur. In paragraph #1, the system is referred to as *DTP*; in the remainder of the article, the acronym *CDP* is used. The switch in terminology is unjustified. Similarly, the article refers to a "primary goal" in paragraph #4, and a "central goal" in the final paragraph; the adjectives seem equivalent, but describe different goals.

A Promotional Publication

This sample of a promotional publication is distributed by the Department of English, Texas A&M University (see Figure 2.5).

Communicative Aim

1. *What does the writer perceive to be the communicative aim?*
The writer perceives the communicative aim as persuasive, describing opportunities for professional writers in order to interest students in the Writing Specialization.
2. *Is the communicative aim clearly identified or explained in the text?*
In the final paragraph, the writer identifies the communicative aim by inviting students to register for the program.
3. *Are there subordinate aims in the text? If so, what are they? Are they appropriate for this text?*
The publication also has a referential aim: to inform students of the program and its requirements.

Audience

1. *Who does the writer perceive to be the primary audience for this text?*
The writer perceives the primary audience is undergraduate students in all disciplines at Texas A&M University, specifically students who normally excel in their writing courses.
2. *Who does the writer perceive to be the secondary audience for this text?*
The writer perceives the secondary audience as academic advisors and instructors who might wish to refer promising students to this program.
3. *Has the writer appropriately analyzed the primary and secondary audiences?*
The writer has appropriately analyzed the audience, with the following exceptions:
a) Students will probably be unfamiliar with specific professional opportunities in writing as well as with the nature of the required courses, and this could deter them from investigating the program.

The Writing Specialization

Texas A&M University

The Writing Specialization is a program designed to give students in business, scientific, technical, or humanistic disciplines eighteen hours of intensive training in a broad range of communication skills. Students who achieve a grade of B or better in all eighteen hours of coursework will receive a certificate signifying their successful completion of this training. Because of the growing demand for highly skilled, professionally competent writers in business, industry, and government, the student with training in writing, speaking, editing, and communication skills has improved job opportunities. Often the individual who possesses such skills gets a job sooner and advances faster—in any profession—than someone without those skills.

> *Author:*
> *Can you offer some specific examples here?*

All students choosing this program will take four core courses: English 210, Argumentation and Composition; English 301, Technical Writing; English 320, Technical Editing; and Speech Communication 404, Technical and Professional Speaking. In addition, the student will select six hours of supporting courses usually connected with the student's major. Students, in consultation with the Writing Specialization Coordinator in the Department of English, can thereby create their own program of special emphasis.

> *Your audience is students and they probably don't know what these courses involve. I think you need to provide some description of each course.*

To register for the The Writing Specialization or to receive more information about it, contact the Writing Specialization Coordinator, Department of English.

> *Author:*
> *Should you be more specific here? Can you give the person's name, office number, and office phone? Students will then have all the needed info.*

Figure 2.5. Editing a promotional publication for accuracy.

b) Students might also expect to receive specific instructions regarding program registration from a promotional publication: the final paragraph violates this expectation. Instead of focusing the students' energy on the investigation of the Writing Specialization, the publication requires students to investigate the identity and location of the Writing Specialization Coordinator.

4. Has the writer invoked the appropriate audience?
The invoked audience is an exclusive group of students interested in pursuing a career in professional writing and attracted to the rigorous requirements of this training or program.

Information Gathering

1. Has the writer gathered appropriate information?
The information is appropriate: it is all pertinent to the subject of the Writing Specialization.

2. Has the writer gathered sufficient information?
Additional information is required in the following cases:
a) In paragraph #1, the general description of the professional opportunities in writing is neither especially informative nor intriguing.
b) In paragraph #2, the writer needs to annotate the course title. Course numbers and titles alone cannot accurately or precisely characterize the program and the training it offers.
c) In paragraph #3, the writer's goal of having interested students contact the Writing Specialization Coordinator is thwarted because crucial information is omitted (e.g., coordinator's name, office number, office phone).

3. Are the information sources reliable?
No information sources are cited.

4. Is the information plausible?
The information seems plausible: it is similar to the requirements of a college minor, and the grade requirement is often characteristic of certification programs.

5. Is the information consistent?
The information is consistent: for example, the required courses would seem to provide adequate preparation for the professional opportunities described.

REFERENCES

1. Aristotle, *Rhetoric*, W. R. Roberts (trans.), The Modern Library, New York, 1954.
2. E. P. J. Corbett, *Classical Rhetoric for the Modern Student*, 2nd edition, Oxford University Press, New York, 1971.
3. J. L. Kinneavy, *A Theory of Discourse*, Norton, New York, 1971.
4. T. Clevinger, Jr., *Audience Analysis*, Bobbs-Merrill, Indianapolis, 1966.
5. C. H. Woolbert, Speaking and Writing—A Study of Differences, *Quarterly Journal of Speech Education, 8*, pp. 271–285, 1922.
6. M. Shaughnessy, *Errors and Expectations*, Oxford University Press, New York, 1977.

7. J. A. DeVito, *The Psychology of Speech and Language*, Random House, New York, 1970.
8. T. M. Sawyer, Why Speech Will Not Totally Replace Writing, *College Composition and Communication, 18*, pp. 43–48, 1977.
9. J. L. M. Trim, Speech Education, in *The Teaching of English*, R. Quirk and A. H. Smith (eds.), Oxford University Press, London, pp. 60–86, 1964.
10. J. C. Mathes and D. W. Stevenson, *Designing Technical Reports*, Bobbs-Merrill, Indianapolis, 1976.
11. L. Flower, *Problem-Solving Strategies for Writing*, 2nd edition, Harcourt Brace Jovanovich, New York, 1985.
12. L. Ede and A. Lunsford, Audience Addressed/Audience Invoked: The Role of Audience in Composition Theory and Pedagogy, *College Composition and Communication, 35*, pp. 155–171, 1984.
13. R. Carosso, *Technical Communications*, Wadsworth, Belmont, CA, 1986.
14. J. W. Ong, The Writer's Audience Is Always a Fiction, *Publication of the Modern Language Association, 90*, pp. 9–21, 1975.
15. K. Burke, The Five Key Terms of Dramatism, in *Contemporary Rhetoric*, W. R. Winterowd (ed.), Harcourt Brace Jovanovich, New York, pp. 183–199, 1975.

CHAPTER 3

Arrangement

RHETORICAL THEORY OF ARRANGEMENT

While gathering information about a subject, the writer is simultaneously beginning the process of organization. The rhetorical canon of *arrangement* refers to this responsibility of the writer. Called *taxis* (e.g., taxonomy) by the Greeks, arrangement in Latin is *dispositio* and involves five major divisions in a persuasive text: *exordium*, the introduction; *narratio*, the facts or circumstances about the subject; *confirmatio*, the rhetor's evidence; *refutatio*, the rhetor's explanation and rejection of opposing opinions; and *peroratio*, the conclusion. Because the ancients considered rhetoric as persuasion, their emphasis on the selection and arrangement of subject matter focuses on the development of these divisions—divisions important for effective forensic rhetoric. For Aristotle, arrangement can be likened to *techne*, an art by which one adapts means to a specific end. Not only should rhetors compose their discourse according to these key segments, but they should also judge carefully the collective effect of these segments.

The Roman rhetorician Cicero also places great value on arrangement, instructing the speaker to be concerned with the order of ideas in light of 1) the nature of the discourse; 2) the nature of the subject (e.g., the quality and quantity of evidence about the subject); 3) the nature or ethos of the speaker (e.g., personality, moral and philosophical biases); and 4) the nature of the audience (e.g., age, social, political, economic, and educational level, disposition at the time) [1, p. 300]. That is, the fashion in which a rhetor organizes a text is determined by the rhetorical situation. According to Cicero, rhetors should consider the effect of arrangement holistically, instead of just focusing analytically on individual sections, especially because the wider perspective allows a superior appreciation of the genuine complexity of the discourse.

Just as the classical rhetoricians show concern for understanding the structure of discourse in order to teach student speakers, so too do the nineteenth-century rhetoricians. One notable figure in the nineteenth century is Alexander

Bain, who popularized the notion that discourse could be categorized into four major modes of discourse: narration, exposition, description, and persuasion. And within these four modes, various methods of paragraph development gain prominence (e.g., comparison–contrast, cause–effect, definition, and classification). For Bain, the paragraph is a type of "macro-sentence" or "meta-sentence" [2, p. 417], which follows six rules:

1. Explicit Reference: The bearing of each sentence upon what precedes shall be explicit and unmistakeable.
2. Parallel Construction: Consecutive sentences that repeat or illustrate the same idea should be formed alike, as far as possible.
3. Topic Sentence: The first sentence, unless obviously preparatory, should indicate the subject of the Paragraph (sic).
4. Consecutive Arrangement: Each statement should follow the plan of the Paragraph (sic) and be in its appropriate place.
5. Overall Unity: A Paragraph (sic) should possess Unity (sic) which implies clarity of purpose and forbids irrelevancies and digressions.
6. Subordination: As in the Sentence (sic), the Paragraph (sic) should maintain a due proportion between the principal subject and subordinate statements [2, p. 413].

Bain's paragraph theory has dominated writers' ways of thinking about the structure of a text.

In response to Bain's notion of paragraphing and modes of discourse, theorists such as Paul Rodgers and Willis Pitkin present discourse structure in terms of discourse stadia [3-5] or discourse blocs [6,7]. While Bain focused on the paragraph as the central unit of composition, these rhetoricians strived to advance discourse theory "beyond the paragraph." According to Rodgers, writers develop ideas through accretion (i.e., coordination) or adjunction (i.e., subordination) to form various stadia of discourse consisting of one paragraph or a series of related paragraphs, depending on the nature of the idea being developed. In his research on discourse structure, Pitkin asserts that the development and movement of a text is accomplished through a hierarchical arrangement of discourse blocs. For both of these theorists, the paragraph is perceived as a constituent of a larger, more important element in the structure of discourse. In effect, researchers such as Rodgers and Pitkin have enabled discourse theorists to understand the whole structure of a text (macrostructure) in terms of its major internal components (microstructures)—a great leap from nineteenth-century to twentieth-century perceptions about arrangement.

In this chapter on arrangement, these larger issues are discussed. To guide writers and editors in the organization of information, we will consider the following: 1) determining the verbal-visual orientation of a text; 2) integrating principles of organization within a text; 3) diagramming a text; 4) establishing coherence and cohesion; and 5) editing for clarity.

Verbal-Visual Orientation

The importance of graphics to the communication of information is widely recognized, especially in the field of technical writing. This recognition, however, has usually been limited to a perception of graphics as "visual aids" designed only following the verbal composition of the text, following the invention and arrangement stages of composing.

This denigration of graphics reveals a verbal bias which aims to "privilege the written word" [8, p. 127] and which erroneously assumes the essay is typical of written communication [9, p. 67]. This verbal bias also proscribes a genuine appreciation of the rhetorical power and scope of visual display: graphics is traditionally perceived as only reinforcing verbal information as opposed to organizing and communicating information, as comprising only figures and tables as opposed to page design, sizes and styles of type, color, headings.

As communications research discovers the merits of integrating verbal and visual display, however, and as the technology which allows and inspires this integration evolves [10, p. 35], previous prejudices yield to a liberating perception of the diversity of written discourse:

We might think of texts arranged along a continuum, from texts at one end which convey relatively little information visually, to texts at the opposite end which reveal substantial information through such visible cues as white space, illustrations, variation in typeface, and use of nonalphabetic symbols, such as numbers, asterisks, and punctuation [9, p. 66].

And just as different texts are more or less visually oriented, so also are different graphics: some visuals require less "reading" (i.e., linear or sequential perception) [11, p. 147]. All tables, for example, require horizontal and vertical reading: the appropriately designed graph or chart, however, communicates its information without this reading. Color is also immediately perceived and requires no reading, similar to boldfacing or changes in typeface and typesize. Headings, however, while immediately seen because of their position on the page, still require reading for comprehension and are, therefore, more verbally oriented than the surrounding white space. Obviously, visually oriented texts employ more visually oriented graphics.

The determination of the visual or verbal orientation of a text is critical to the composition of a text, especially to the arrangement stage of composing. In this determination, the writer considers the ideas arrived at during the invention stage of composing and decides the verbal/visual display of those ideas according to seven guidelines on the communicative characteristics of the discourse and the receptive characteristics of the intended audience:

1. The more instructive or persuasive a text, the more likely it is to require a visual presentation of information: that is, seeing is believing. The more strictly informative a text, the more likely it is to rely on verbal presentation [12, p. 276; 13, pp. 78-82].
2. Texts requiring the reader's immediate attention are more likely to employ a visual presentation of information because "reading" is never as quick as "seeing," (i.e., visuals heighten the efficiency of communication.) The less pressing is the need to examine a text, the more likely it is for that text to be exclusively verbal [12, pp. 270-271].
3. Texts intended for random access are more likely to employ a visual presentation of information. The more sequential a text, the more likely it is to rely on a verbal presentation of information because verbal explanation is itself linear and sequential [9, p. 76; 14, pp. 33-37].
4. The less motivated the intended reader of a text is assumed to be, the more likely that text is to employ a visual display of information as a way to motivate the intended reader (e.g., because visuals solicit "seeing" as opposed to "reading," visually oriented texts seem easier to enter). The more motivated the intended reader, the more likely the text is to be exclusively verbal [9, p. 76].
5. The less educated the reader, the more likely is a visual presentation of information. Because higher education typically yields better verbal skills, a strictly verbal presentation of information is usually reserved for the educated reader [15, pp. 480-481; 16, pp. 507-510].
6. The less familiar with the subject the reader is, the more critical is a visual presentation of information. Verbal presentation of information is sufficient to stimulate the familiar reader's visual memory of the subject. Readers unfamiliar with a subject have no appropriate visual memory and are therefore more likely to require a visual presentation of information [15, pp. 480-481; 17, pp. 4-5].
7. The more distracting the reader's environment, the more important the immediate and simultaneous perception which a visual presentation of information allows. A quiet environment is more conducive to the slower, sequential perception required with the verbal presentation of information [14, p. 391].

Specific exceptions to each of the seven generalizations occur immediately to the experienced writer (e.g., while designed for sequential access, procedures usually incorporate extensive visuals; while a technical description is primarily informative, it typically requires detailed illustration). The occurrence of exceptions to the seven generalizations, however, emphasizes the importance of considering all seven factors in the determination of the visual or verbal orientation of a given text. In addition, exceptions clarify the reason that a given text is visually or verbally oriented. For example, it is not the communicative access which orients a set of procedures to visual display, but the instructive aim of the discourse. Conversely, it is not the aim of the discourse which orients a technical description to the visual, but its random access.

This choice of verbal or visual orientation is crucial: it is the writer's and editor's initial decision on arrangement and guides their rhetorical choices on style and delivery.

Principles of Organization

It is the editor's responsibility to insure that the writer has selected the clearest method of organization, given the communicative aim and audience of the discourse. There are two major ways to organize the components of a document: sequentially and categorically.

Sequential Organization

To develop ideas sequentially means that writers may use *spatial, chronological*, or *hierarchical* patterns to arrange their information. A characteristic common to all of these methods of organization is their predictability (i.e., the reader, given the initial piece of information in the sequence, is able to predict or anticipate how the subsequent piece of information will connect to it).

Spatial organization is a reader's logical expectation for the arrangement of descriptive information. This pattern of organization progresses in a single direction (e.g., moving from the top of the object to the bottom of the object, or left to right, or east to west, or north to south). By moving in one direction in the description of the object, the writer makes it easy for the reader to comprehend and assimilate the descriptive information being conveyed. Each new piece of information develops the preceding piece of information in a predictable and linear fashion.

Violation of this expectation makes it more difficult for the reader to understand the document. If, for example, in describing an object, a writer started the description in the middle, moved up toward the top, then down toward the bottom, then up to the top, then down toward the middle again, the reader would find it impossible to predict or anticipate what portion of the object the next piece of information would describe. It is also possible to reinforce this spatial organization of the verbal discussion through appropriate visuals (e.g., photographs, blueprints, organizational charts, and representational drawings with exploded or cutaway views).

Chronological organization is appropriate to a document narrating a process or explaining a procedure. Chronological organization moves either forward or backward through time. In a set of instructions, for example, the steps are always listed in their order of performance. In a resume, however, job experience is usually given in reverse chronological order, with the most recent job listed first. Arranging information in this single direction makes it easy for the reader to anticipate and assimilate each new piece of information given: that is, each new step in the procedure can be added to the preceding step as the reader builds his or her understanding of the total procedure. Chronological organization is the reader's logical expectation for narrative or instructive material, and violation of this expectation makes it more difficult for the reader to comprehend the document. If, for example, a job applicant lists previous work experience in random order, the reader will find it difficult to develop a clear sense of this person's employment history. Or imagine a set of instructions in which the steps are *not* given in the order in which they are performed. It is also possible to reinforce this chronological organization of the verbal discussion with appropriate visuals (e.g., numbered or alphabetized lists, flow charts, storyboards, line graphs, time lapse photographs, and sequential drawings).

Hierarchical organization is the organizational method a writer is likely to choose for a document which will include conclusions and recommendations. This pattern of organization moves in either ascending or descending order. For example, in identifying the factors which justify a candidate's promotion, a writer might list achievements in ascending order of importance, culminating in the most impressive and persuasive accomplishments of the candidate. Or, in listing grievances, a writer might begin with the most serious complaint for dramatic emphasis and end with the least serious. Again, by moving in one direction, from more important to least important or vice versa, the writer signals to the reader what each new piece of information contributes to the information previously given. Hierarchical organization is a reader's logical expectation for listing of causes, effects, costs, benefits, similarities, differences, advantages, and disadvantages, especially when such information is being listed for persuasive purposes. A writer's failure to provide this type of organization may result in a document with a less convincing set of conclusions and recommendations. For example, with recommendations listed in random order, the reader will find it difficult to determine which of the recommendations is most beneficial or urgent, and therefore, which recommendation to implement immediately. Because the writer has abdicated the responsibility in logically ordering recommendations, the reader is forced to assume the writer's responsibility: the reader may be unwilling or unable to do this effectively. And, as a consequence, the reader may begin to question the writer's credibility and competence altogether. This hierarchical organization of the verbal discussion can be reinforced with appropriate visuals (e.g., numbered or alphabetized lists, pie charts, bull's eye charts, and multiple-line graphs.

Categorical Organization

To develop ideas categorically is to design *comparative* or *causal* patterns of information. The writer establishes categories of information (e.g., similarities and differences, causes and effects, advantages and disadvantages) and either discusses one entire category at a time or alternates between the categories, covering one piece of information from each category until all information has been provided. For example, in a feasibility study on a computer system, a writer might choose to discuss all the advantages and then all the disadvantages or each advantage and its corresponding disadvantage.

Categorical organization might also be combined with sequential organization: (e.g., the writer might discuss all the advantages in order of importance, and then all the disadvantages in order of importance). Because categorical organization is without the single linear direction of sequential organization, readers find it a more complicated pattern: that is, it is more difficult for readers to predict or anticipate information categorically organized. As a consequence, it is especially important that writers continually signal their chosen direction with transitional words and phrases. Categorical organization is reinforced through appropriate visuals (e.g., paired listings, paired photos or drawings, tables, and bar graphs).

Diagramming the Discourse

The principles of organization occur either in isolation or in combination. Discourse might thus develop according to a simple principle of organization (i.e., chronological, spatial, hierarchical, or categorical) or according to a complex principle of organization (i.e., hierarchical-chronological, hierarchical-spatial, hierarchical-categorical).

These principles of organization give direction and structure to a text. Six basic structures are possible, and each is easily visualized or diagrammed [18, pp. 218-233].

Line

A text which has a line structure progresses in a single direction without interruption or digression. It begins at one point and ends at another, taking the reader on a simple journey. A line structure is the result of a writer using one of the three sequential principles of organization. For example, a writer might chronologically organize a series of instructions, and the text would progress in linear fashion from the first step in the procedure. Or a writer might spatially organize a description of a machine, moving from the top of the object to the bottom of the object or vice versa. Or a writer might hierarchically organize a causal analysis of a mechanical malfunction, starting with the most important cause and ending with the least important cause or vice versa.

Circle

A text which has a circle structure returns to the point at which it began, taking the reader on a round trip. The journey is through space or time, and a circle structure thus requires either a spatial or chronological organization. For example, if a writer is describing a looping or repetitive procedure, the final instruction must return the reader to the initial instruction. Or a writer's description of the interior of a house might lead the reader from the entrance, through each room in the house, and back to the entrance.

Pyramid

A text which has a pyramid structure progresses forward and outward simultaneously, expanding its perspective from the specific to the general, covering more and more territory as it goes. It takes the reader on a journey from the narrow and concrete to the global and abstract. A pyramid structure is the result of a writer using spatial or chronological organization within a hierarchical organization. For example, a writer might design a set of instructions to progress in order of difficulty, and the reader would thus learn simple procedures before learning complicated procedures; the step-by-step explanation of each procedure would be organized chronologically. Or a writer might design a description to progress hierarchically from the parts to the whole: the description at each point in the progression would be organized spatially, covering the object from top to bottom or left to right or vice versa.

Funnel

A funnel structure is the opposite of a pyramid structure: a text with a funnel structure progresses from the general to the specific, narrowing its perspective, defining its scope more and more precisely. The journey here is from the broad and expansive to the focused and finite. A funnel structure is the result of using a spatial or chronological organization within a hierarchical organization. For example, a writer might design a set of instructions to progress in order of frequency or performance, covering routine procedures before explaining specialized procedures: the steps involved in the performance of each procedure would be chronologically organized. Or a writer might design a description of a mechanism to progress from the whole to the parts: the description of each point in the progression would have a spatial organization.

String-of-Beads

A text which has a string-of-beads structure is episodic: it is a series of associated ideas without a clear and necessary direction or progression. The reader's journey is essentially a meandering from stopping point to stopping point. A string-of-beads structure proscribes the three kinds of sequential organization and requires categorical organization in episodic fashion. For example, if a writer is describing the benefits of a product, categorical organization in the form of a bulleted list might be a wise rhetorical choice: different users of the product might place a different priority on particular benefits and therefore reject a hierarchical organization in the form of a numbered list. The categorical organization has flexibility: it is adaptable to different readers.

Braid

A braid structure integrates several ideas or perspectives within a single discourse, and the reader's journey is therefore circuitous and complex. A braid structure is the result of using a categorical organization of alternating design: the writer weaves together the various threads of the discussion, the various aspects of the subject. For example, in a comparative analysis, a writer might assess three alternatives against five criteria and organize the discussion according to those criteria. That is, the writer might identify and explain the first criterion, discuss how each alternative satisfies that criterion, and proceed in the same fashion for the remaining criteria.

Coherence and Cohesion

"A reader normally expects coherence and takes it for granted that there is a connection between sentences that occur sequentially in a speech or in writing" [19, p. 653]. That is, in the process of reading a sentence, readers ask themselves two questions: "What is the meaning of this sentence?" and "What is the relationship between this sentence and earlier sentences?" The longer it takes a reader to answer *both* of these questions, the more difficult the sentence is to understand. This is the case with all levels of discourse (e.g., reading a paragraph requires the determination of its meaning and its relevance to previous paragraphs). Coherence is thus the consequence of cohesive devices and of positioning as well as phrasing, of both visual and verbal techniques.

Coherence is established verbally in five major ways:

- repetition
- substitution

- logical equivalence
- parallelism
- transitions

Repetition

This is the use of the same word or words to reinforce, explain, or develop ideas covered earlier. Repetition is the simplest and clearest way to signal to a reader that a subject discussed before is still being discussed and thus to bring unity and cohesion to a block of discourse. In technical writing, for example, it is especially important that writers employ consistent terminology for objects or ideas: readers are less likely to suffer confusion if a new piece of information always carries the identical name or label. For example, in a computer user's manual, it would be confusing if the *computer display unit* were variously referred to as the *screen, display unit, TV monitor, computer monitor, TV screen, display screen, cathode ray tube*, or *CRT*.

Substitution

This is the use of pronouns and synonyms to refer to previously mentioned ideas and, in doing so, to avoid simple repetition of those earlier ideas and establish a cohesive block of discourse. For example, in the previous sentence, the words *in doing so* and *those earlier* are substitutes which allow the reader to see the connection between information that is currently being given and information that has been given: that is, *in doing so* substitutes for *refers to previously mentioned ideas*, and *those earlier* substitutes for *previously mentioned*.

Pronouns and synonyms are effective only if the words for which they substitute or to which they refer are immediately clear to readers. If a writer is doubtful of this, then repetition of the original word or words is more effective in establishing cohesion.

Logical Equivalence

This way of achieving coherence allows a writer to exploit the implications and inferences of information previously given: that is, the writer assumes this implied or inferred information is understood and requires no additional mention or explanation. In immediately following passages, the writer refers to this information without using repetition or substitution. For example, a writer might compose the following:

The accident occurred at 9 o'clock. The victims died on the way to the hospital.

This is a cohesive sequence of sentences because the word *accident* allows the reader to interpret the word *victims* as the equivalent of *people who experience injuries during accidents.* Equivalence is, however, more difficult and time consuming for readers than either substitution or repetition [20, pp. 21-23], and writers must determine that their readers are capable of bridging between that which is stated and that which is implied.

Parallelism

This is the use of syntactic similarity to establish an equivalent relationship among all items in a series, thus reinforcing the cohesion of the listed items. The syntactic similarity might be that all items in the series are verbs, or nouns, or participles, or prepositional phrases, or *that* clauses, or imperative sentences: all that is necessary is enough syntactic similarity to construct a pattern which readers will recognize easily and understand readily.

Transitions

The function of transitions is to explicitly link two successive words, phrases, clauses, sentences, paragraphs, or blocks of discourse with a clear identification of the relationship between the two. Transitions are of several kinds:

Additive:	in addition, also, moreover, furthermore
Temporal:	meanwhile, while, during, before, after, since
Locative:	above, below, adjacent to, perpendicular to
Enumerative:	first, second, lastly, finally
Comparative:	similarly, likewise, in the same manner
Contrastive:	however, on the other hand, although, whereas, while
Causal:	therefore, as a consequence, hence, thus, since, because
Illustrative:	for example, namely, such as, thus
Explanatory:	that is, in other words
Summative:	in conclusion, in short, to summarize, finally

Cohesion is also achieved visually through the design of headings. The position of headings on a page as well as the typographic size and value (i.e., lightness/darkness) of the headings signals either a coordinate or subordinate relationship between the designated sections of a text. For example, two headings given in the same size of type, in all upper case letters, and in boldface obviously identify coordinated or equally important sections of a text; however, a heading in upper and lower case letters is clearly subordinate to a heading in all upper case letters.

Visual cohesive techniques also have a hierarchical organization. The larger and darker the heading, the more important is its corresponding section of the text. Similarly, a centered heading is more important than a flush left heading, which is more important than an indented heading.

Editing for Clarity

Editing for clarity requires the editor to examine the effectiveness of a writer's rhetorical choices regarding the arrangement of the text. Specifically, the editor assesses the three factors which determine the effectiveness of that arrangement: visual-verbal orientation, organization, and coherence and cohesion.

Visual-Verbal Orientation

Initially, the editor must review the writer's determination of the verbal-visual orientation of the text. A quick and simple way to accomplish this is through answering the following survey of seven considerations (see Figure 3.1). After rating each factor on a scale of 1-5, the writer figures the score for all seven factors: the lowest possible score is 7 and the highest possible score is 35. The higher the score, the more visually oriented the text. The following are general interpretations of the scores:

29-35   primarily visual, using charts and graphs, symbols, diagrams, photographs, color, a variety of type sizes, a minimum of straight text

22-28   visual/verbal, using charts and graphs, diagrams, photographs, color, type in various sizes to distinguish blocks of information, an equal or lesser amount of text

15-21   verbal/visual, using more tables than figures, some color, type in various sizes to distinguish blocks of information, an equal or greater amount of text

7-14   primarily verbal, possibly using some tables, possibly some type in various sizes to distinguish blocks of information, little or no color, most if not all straight text

For example, consider an article in a professional journal. The discourse aim is typically a mix of the informative and persuasive: a score of 3. The discourse urgency is low because critical information would probably be communicated through a widely disseminated daily publication: a score of 1 is therefore appropriate. The discourse access is sequential, a score of 1: articles in professional journals are typically designed to be read from beginning to end. It seems fair to estimate the reader's motivation is fairly high, a score of 2: the reader must choose to read this article and is therefore probably somewhat interested in the subject, especially as the article has some relevance to the reader's professional discipline. The reader of a professional journal is also likely to have advanced education: a score of 2. The reader's familiarity with the subject is likely to be high: a score of 2. The reader's environment is also likely to be relatively quiet

1. Discourse Aim	1 informative	2	3	4	5 persuasive/ instructive
2. Discourse Urgency	1 no immediate attention required	2	3	4	5 immediate attention required
3. Discourse Access	1 sequential	2	3	4	5 random
4. Reader's Motivation	1 motivated	2	3	4	5 unmotivated
5. Reader's Education	1 educated: > 16 years of school	2	3	4	5 uneducated: < 12 years of school
6. Reader's Familiarity with Subject	1 familiar	2	3	4	5 unfamiliar
7. Reader's Environment	1 no distractions/ interruptions	2	3	4	5 numerous distractions/ interruptions

Figure 3.1. Verbal-visual orientation survey.

and undisturbed because this kind of reading is usually reserved for the office or library: a score of 2. The total score for this text then is 13 or primarily verbal. This seems to correspond with the composition of professional journals: mostly straight text, some headings and subheadings, an occasional table, chart, or graph.

Consider also a menu for a family restaurant. The discourse aim is a mix of the informative and the persuasive, identifying the food selections available in a manner that is enticing: a score of 4. The discourse urgency might be considered a 3: it is desirable for the menu to identify the food selections fairly quickly and easily in order to encourage a rapid decision by the customers. The discourse access is random, a score of 5: the typical menu permits reading in any order or sequence, allowing the customer to jump back and forth between pages, between categories of food, between food selections. The reader's motivation is relatively high, a score of 2: the customers of the typical family restaurant, hungry parents and equally hungry children, are primarily interested in eating food as opposed to enjoying a pleasant evening in a romantic or luxurious atmosphere; they are interested in the food selections on the menu and interested in making a choice from the menu selections, especially because the sooner this decision is made, the sooner the food will arrive. Level of education will differ widely: a score of 3. Most customers probably have some familiarity with the type of food served at family restaurants, but may have little or no familiarity with the specific food selections at a particular restaurant: a score of 2. The reader's environment will quite likely be distracting, with the noise of dishes and silverware in use, with other customers talking, with waiters and waitresses taking orders, serving food, cleaning tables: a score of 5. The total score for this text then is 24, visual/verbal, and this corresponds with typical menus of family restaurants: substantial text in small blocks, various sizes and designs of type to identify these blocks of information, bullets to identify the individual items listed, and numerous illustrations or photographs of the food selections.

Organization

The editor must also determine that the writer has adopted the principle(s) of organization for the text appropriate to both the audience and the communicative aim of the discourse. For example, a computer user's manual designed to orient and instruct the inexperienced might be hierarchically organized (i.e., initially covering instructions on common or routine procedures and progressing to instructions on uncommon or specialized procedures). A user's manual designed to serve only as a reference guide for the experienced, however, might be categorically organized (i.e., grouping all procedures according to their function).

A significant aid to the editor's examination of a text's organization is the discourse diagram. This gives the editor a quick perspective on the design of the discourse. Using the general guidelines that follow (see Table 3.1), the editor first decides which of six basic diagrams is appropriate to the audience and communicative aim of the discourse and then insures that the writer's text exhibits the necessary organization. This visualization of a text's organization also aids the editor's evaluation of the coherence and cohesion of the text. This is because a string-of-beads structure or braid structure are inherently less cohesive organizations and require more explicit cohesive devices.

The editor must also determine that all visuals reinforce the desired principle(s) of organization. (See Table 3.2.)

Coherence and Cohesion

The final consideration in the editor's evaluation of the clarity of a text is coherence and cohesion. The editor must examine the discourse for the effectiveness of its repetition, substitution, and equivalence (i.e., the implicit cohesive techniques which establish given/new chains of information). Given/new chains are three possible sequences of information that occur in cohesive discourse. In all given/new chains, new information is linked only to given

Table 3.1. Discourse Diagrams

Discourse Diagram	Principles of Organization
Line	Spatial Chronological Hierarchical
Circle	Spatial Chronological
Pyramid	Hierarchical-Spatial Hierarchical-Chronological
Funnel	Hierarchical-Spatial Hierarchical-Chronological
String of beads	Categorical Hierarchical-Categorical
Braid	Categorical Hierarchical-Categorical

Table 3.2. Organization and Graphics

Principles of Organization	Corresponding Graphics
Spatial	Photographs
	Blueprints
	Organizational charts
	Representational drawings
Chronological	Numbered or alphabetized lists
	Flow charts
	Storyboards
	Line graphs
	Time lapse photographs
	Sequential drawings
Hierarchical	Numbered or alphabetized lists
	Pie charts
	Multiple-line graphs
	Bull's eye charts
	Organizational charts
Categorical	Paired listings
	Paired photographs
	Paired drawings
	Tables
	Bar graphs

information (i.e., information previously mentioned or information assumed to be previously known). Once new information has been linked to given information, the new information is itself considered given, and it is possible to link additional new information to it. Thus every sentence has given and new information, and the new information in each sentence is the given information in subsequent sentences.

The three types of given/new chains are

1) ab	2) ab	3) ab
ac	bc	bc
ad	cd	ad

In the following example of the ab–ac–ad chain, both substitution and repetition have been used to maintain the given information.

Joan Smith, the manager of Compurobics Inc., has requested a meeting with all technicians. Ms. Smith has received numerous customer complaints. She believes that this meeting will help to improve customer service.

The given information is the same throughout, allowing the writer to introduce new information incrementally. This chain is appropriate for readers who might find the information especially difficult.

An example of the second chain is

> The manager of Compurobics Inc. has requested a meeting with all technicians. The technicians have caused numerous customer complaints. This customer dissatisfaction has resulted in decreased sales.

Here, the writer has used repetition and substitution to create an ab-bc cd chain. This alternating pattern is especially appropriate for a general audience. Unlike the earlier ab-ac-ad chain, the given information here is different in each sentence, making reading more difficult. In the ab-bc-cd chain, however, because the new information of one sentence is the given information of the next, relationships between consecutive sentences are still explicit and information thus accessible.

Equivalence has been used in the series of sentences below that illustrate an ab-bc-ad chain:

> Ms. Smith, manager of Compurobics Inc., has requested a meeting with all technicians. Customer service has been unsatisfactory. Ms. Smith believes that this meeting will help to improve sales.

This is a mix of the earlier ab-ac-ad and ab-bc-cd chains, sometimes using the same given information in consecutive sentences and sometimes using the new information of one sentence as the given information of the next. The variety and complexity of this organization is especially appropriate to readers either familiar with the subject or willing to expend additional effort to understand the text.

The editor must decide which of the three chains is appropriate to a passage and then insure the passage exhibits that given/new chain. In addition, the editor must determine that the writer has incorporated sufficient and appropriate transitions to reinforce, emphasize, or clarify the implicit cohesive linking of given/new chains. This is especially important for categorically organized texts because of their absence of implicit direction: that is, a sequentially organized text proceeds in a clear and obvious direction, whereas a categorically organized text is either episodic or alternating and thus more difficult for readers to anticipate and assimilate their information.

The writer must also examine the text for the parallel wording and phrasing of all ideas and objects in a series, including the wording and phrasing of headings. The editor must determine that the semantic comparability of paired or listed items is reinforced through their syntactic comparability.

Finally, the editor must also examine the text for the effectiveness of its visual cohesion techniques. Using the following guide to the hierarchy of heading

Table 3.3. Hierarchy of Heading Designs

Size	Value	Position
1. Enlarged uppercase	1. Bold, underlined	1. Centered
2. Enlarged upper/lower case	2. Bold	2. Flush left
3. Text-size uppercase	3. Regular, underlined	3. Indented
4. Text-size upper/lower case	4. Regular	

designs (see Table 3.3), the editor checks the headings in a text and finds their corresponding three-digit number. The lower the number, the more important the heading (e.g., 111 versus 443). Coordinated headings have the same numbers; subordinated headings have higher numbers. The editor must assess the relationship among the various sections of the text and insure that the design of each heading appropriately signals the desired coordinate or subordinate relationship.

PRACTICE

In editing as well as writing, theory informs and inspires practice. In this section, we will again examine three major types of texts: technical publications, news publications, and promotional publications.

To aid the editor in thoroughly and logically evaluating the writer's arrangement techniques apparent in the text, we have developed the following heuristic (see Figure 3.2). This series of questions can guide the editor through an analysis of the arrangement within a text and allow the editor to identify specific problems therein. As a heuristic, the Editor's Arrangement Inventory is designed to be recursive and flexible.

Using this inventory, the editor can locate problems in the text and either determine the necessary solutions to these problems or suggest that the writer improve the visual or verbal arrangement of the text. Comments and suggestions to the author, usually phrased as questions, again require small slips of paper (e.g., 3M Post-It Notes). In addition to these author queries, the editor might change the organization of the text directly, using appropriate editing symbols (see Table 3.4).

In the following samples of technical, news, and promotional publications, we will illustrate how the application of the Editor's Arrangement Inventory yields appropriate author queries and edited text.

Table 3.4. Editing Symbols for Clarity

in the text	in the margin	explanation
treasurer elected on Tuesday ∧	∧	insert
asked us a question	↲	delete
of the book. ⁋She also	⁋	start new paragraph
⌐Introduction	(fl)	move flush left
page 75⌐	(fl rt)	move flush right
with us.⟩ He has always	(run in)	run in with preceding line: no line break or new paragraph
⌉ Recommendations ⌊	⊐⊏	center horizontally
Figure 1	⊢⊣	center vertically
symbols words	═══	align horizontally
Labor ‖= $75 Parts ‖= $39	‖	align vertically
discussion	(cap)	change to upper case
History	(lc)	change to lower case
A Theory of Discourse	(ital)	change to italics
List of Illustrations	(bf)	change to boldface
vice versa	(rom)	change to roman (i.e., plain)

Verbal-Visual Orientation
1. What does the writer perceive to be the verbal-visual orientation of the text? 2. Is this orientation appropriate?

Principles and Diagrams of Organization
1. What is the organization of the discourse? Spatial? Chronological? Hierarchical? Categorical? 2. How might the text be diagrammed? Line? Circle? Pyramid? Funnel? String of Beads? Braid? 3. Is this organization appropriate to the aim of the discourse? Does it serve to clarify the information? 4. Is the organization appropriate to the audience of the discourse? Does it help readers to assimilate the information?

Coherence and Cohesion
1. Does the writer establish a chain of given/new information? Is this chain achieved through repetition, substitution, or equivalence? 2. Does the writer use sufficient and appropriate transitions? 3. Does the writer use parallel wording and phrasing as necessary? 4. Does the writer use sufficient and appropriate headings? Are the coordinate and subordinate headings clearly and logically ordered? 5. Do the size, value, and position of headings clearly indicate their degree of importance?

Figure 3.2. Editor's arrangement inventory.

A Technical Publication

This sample is excerpted from a research report intended for publication in a professional journal (see Figure 3.3).

Verbal-Visual Orientation

1. What does the writer perceive to be the verbal-visual orientation of the discourse?
The writer perceives the research report as verbally oriented: it is exclusively uninterrupted text.
2. Is this orientation appropriate?
With the exception of discourse access, the writer has appropriately identified

Evaluation   page 15

Writing Apprehension   RESULTS AND DISCUSSION

Curiously, students in both the control (N=52) and
the experimental (N=103)groups showed significant increases on the Daly-Miller Writing Apprehension Test
(1975) across the semester (t=-2.21, t=-2.16, p<.05; mean
pretest vs. posttest: control= 72.5, 76.2; experimen-
tal=68.7, 72.3). The small but signifcant increases in
apprehension were clearly not expected, and, perhaps
equally important, did not distinguish between the control and experimental group.

To test for the possibility that the Daly-Miller,
as a whole, was not sensitive enough to pick up differences in students' attitudes toward evaluation of their
writing, a subscale of ten items was created from that
test. These ten items--1, 2, 4, 6, 12, 18, 22, and 25--
all probe students' attitudes about having others read
their writing and about having their essays evaluated.

Two interesting questions emerge by considering the
subscale results where students' overall apprehension
increased but their apprehension about evaluation decreased: Is writing apprehension a single monolithic
entity that the Daly-Miller assumes it is? And how sensitive is this test as an indicator of apprehension?

move to page 16

While the control group did not show significant
decreases on these ten items (t=0.86, p.>01; mean pretest
versus posttest=32.3, 31.9), the experimental group improved significantly (t=2.68, p<.01; mean pretest versus
posttest = 32.6, 31.7). Student writers in the experimental group liked positively the one-to-one conferences
in which they discussed their writing and suggestions for
guided revision with their instructors. Student writers
became more comfortable and confident about the evaluation process in the experimental group when their essays
were rated the same by two outside readers. The rater
agreement and guidelines for revision seemed to put these

Author:

This statistical information might be more accessible and clear if it were in table form.

Author:

Subheadings in this section would give the reader a better sense of the order and relationship of ideas.

Author:

This paragraph needs to follow the paragraph on results.

Author:

Again, this statistical info would be easier to grasp in table form.

Figure 3.3.   Editing a technical publication for clarity.

Evaluation   page 16

move from page 15

student writers at more ease about writing for other readers and turning in essays for evaluation.

Writing Quality

Control group essays were graded in the traditional
manner; experimental group essays were simultaneously
evaluated holistically. These Two different procedures
were used for determining writing quality in the two
groups. This difference in grading coupled with the fact
that different topics for the expressive, referential, and
persuasive essays were used to measure pre- and post-
course writing quality make it impossible to compare the
two groups directly. Improvement over the semester can be
at least estimated by comparing grades on an early and
later paper for the control group and by comparing holistic scores of an early and a later paper for the experimental group, nevertheless.

In the first case, the results seemed valid in light
of the fact that the instructors' grades were purely dependent on the perceived quality of the writing (that is,
not influenced by pedagogical considerations) and the
writing tasks chosen from the beginning and end of the
semester made roughly the same demands on the student
writers. In the second case, the results seemed valid in
light of the fact that the raters evaluated the pre- and
post-essays on the same scale and the writing tasks were
equivalent. Given the results' validity, the data suggest
that both groups improved significantly in writing quality
over the semester.

The control group showed some increase in writing
quality from the expressive essay to the persuasive essay
(t= -0.42, p>.01). However, the experimental group made
extraordinary progress from essay 1 to essay 5 (t=-3.01,
p<.01). Again, while the grades of students whose work
had been evaluated traditionally steadily increased, their
progress was not near the increase in quality that students whose writing had been evaluated by summative and
formative techniques. The guided revision and one-to-one

Author:

Another table is in order here, don't you think?

Figure 3.3. Editing a technical publication for clarity (cont'd)

```
Evaluation                                        page 17


conferencing seemed  to significantly increase the writ-
ing abilities of students.
         To measure the reliability of raters of the experi-
mental group's essays, a Spearman's Rho (i.e., a type of
correlation between rank order data) was used.  The cor-
relation coefficients for each of the five essays were
determined (#1=.39; #2=.54; #3=.74; #4=.67; #5=.58) and
averaged.  The average of the coefficients is .58, a fair
correlation. According to Diederich, for example, a cor-
relation such as .67 is "far from satisfactory, but it is
typical. ... I have rarely been able to boost the average
correlation between pairs of readers above .50, and other
examiners tell me that this is about what they get" (33).
```

Figure 3.3.   Editing a technical publication for clarity (cont'd).

the verbal-visual orientation (see Figure 3.4); because the reader of a research report will likely require random access to the information, the writer might seriously consider integrating subheadings and tables.

Principles and Diagrams of Organization

1. *What is the principle of organization?*
The research report has a complex organization, using categorical and sequential principles. In this excerpt, for example, the writer has divided the research findings into two groups: the results on writing apprehension and the results on writing quality. Within each division, the writer establishes a sequence of identifying the data and then explaining them; however, paragraph #3 violates this sequence.
2. *How might the text be diagrammed?*
This excerpt of the research report might be visualized as a string-of-beads: the equivalency of the two topics allows either ordering (i.e., writing apprehension and writing quality, or vice versa). Within the discussion of the topics, however, a pyramid diagram is effective: specific data leads to general interpretations. Because paragraph #3 is the most general interpretation drawn from the findings on writing apprehension, it might be easier to understand if it occurred at the end of this section of the report.

1. Discourse Aim 1 (2) 3 4 5
informative   persuasive/
                               instructive
research report focusing on data, persuasive subordinate aim

2. Discourse Urgency (1) 2 3 4 5
no immediate   immediate
attention   attention
required   required
appearing in professional journal, published quarterly

3. Discourse Access 1 2 3 (4) 5
sequential   random
*reader will wish to locate specific blocks of information as necessary,
jumping around in the text, skipping sections, using other sections for
later reference and info retrieval*

4. Reader's Motivation 1 (2) 3 4 5
motivated   unmotivated
*probably, because subject is pertinent to reader's field, assuming
active professional who tries to remain current with the discipline*

5. Reader's Education (1) 2 3 4 5
educated: uneducated:
> 16 years   < 12 years
of school   of school
normally

**6. Reader's Familiarity
with Subject** 1 (2) 3 4 5
familiar   unfamiliar
*probably, because reader is a professional in the field and has at least
above average understanding or knowledge of the subject*

7. Reader's Environment (1) 2 3 4 5
no   numerous
distractions/   distractions/
interruptions   interruptions
office or library, during periods of studious activity

Figure 3.4. Verbal-visual orientation survey for the technical publication.

3. *Is this organization appropriate to the aim of the discourse? Does it serve to clarify the information?*

This organization is appropriate to the referential aim of the discourse: the writer is systematically grouping information, reporting it, and explaining it. This is normal for a research report.

4. *Is this organization appropriate to the audience of the discourse? Does it help readers to assimilate the information?*

The organization is appropriate to the audience: researchers in the field of composition and rhetoric will probably consider the categorization of topics (i.e., writing apprehension and writing quality) as sensible and standard for the field. The readers will undoubtedly expect to see both a presentation and explication of the numerical results; in addition, based on their familiarity with the conventions of research reports, the readers will here expect to see the numerical data displayed in tables for easier assimilation.

Coherence and Cohesion

1. *Does the writer establish a chain of given/new information? Is this chain achieved through repetition, substitution, or equivalence?*

The writer establishes a given/new ab-bc-cd chain in the section on writing apprehension, using repetition and substitution. This chain breaks with paragraph #3, which assumes that new information (i.e., the subscale findings) is given. In the section on writing quality, similarly, the opening sentence is given information. In this section also, the writer uses a variety of given/ new chains; as a consequence, logical equivalence as well as repetition and substitution occur.

2. *Does the writer use sufficient and appropriate transitions?*

Transitions prove especially necessary to the section on writing quality, given its complex series of given/new information chains. The writer seems to be sensitive to the difficulty that readers might have in negotiating this portion of the text: transitions are frequent and fitting.

3. *Does the writer use parallel wording and phrasing as necessary?*

The writer uses parallel wording and phrasing to clarify information as necessary (e.g., the opening coordinated sentence of the writing quality section).

4. *Does the writer use sufficient and appropriate headings? Are the coordinate and subordinate headings clearly and logically ordered?*

The writer uses headings, but no subheadings. The reader is therefore given unnecessarily limited access to the information.

5. *Do the size, value, and position of headings clearly indicate their degree of importance?*

The all upper case, underlined, and centered major headings of the research report will dominate the upper/lower case, underlined, and flush left subheadings inserted for each major subsection.

Electronic Publishing and <u>Texas Liberal Review</u>

no¶

→ Instead of having the Texas State Printing Center typeset articles for the <u>Texas Liberal Review</u>, we plan, now that word processors are so widely used, to capture authors' keystrokes whenever possible. With funds from both TALCI and Texas State University, we have purchased equipment that should allow us to produce galley proofs of <u>TLRev</u> in the editorial office without having to pay for typesetting services. The savings should be substantial, allowing TALCI to recoup its investment in less than a year.

Continuity will mark upcoming issues of the <u>TLRev</u>, even as we move away from old-fashioned typesetting to desk-top publishing in producing the journal. If all goes as planned, the spring 1988 issue will match the style, format, and quality of earlier issues while at the same time being produced by radically different means.

~~System Description~~

For those interested in a detailed description of the equipment ("robot talk" as one of our colleagues calls it), we have a Compaq Deskpro 286 computer (with a 30 megabyte hard drive and a 5-1/4 inch floppy disk drive), an Apple LaserWriter Plus printer, a full-page portrait monitor, and a Microsoft serial mouse. The software for our system runs on the MS-DOS Version 3 operating system. We will be using WordPositor word processing software in conjunction with the PositivePublisher page layout software. Those authors who create electronic manuscripts processed in WordPositor (MS-DOS, 5-1/4 inch floppy) will produce material most compatible with our system; however, we should be able to accomodate any document converted to a DOS/ASCII file.

~~Conclusion~~

More information will be supplied at a later date as we learn about our abilities (and inabilities) to convert files from various word processing programs, from different operating systems, and from several sizes of microcomputer discs. Until further notice, all authors—those who work at typewriters and those who work at word processors—should continue to submit two paper ("hard") copies of manuscripts for evaluation by readers. Once an article is accepted, we will request a disk from the author if the work was prepared on a word processor.

Margin annotations:

Author:
If available and if space allows, a photo displaying the new desktop publishing equipment might accompany this article.

Author:
Why not make this the 1st paragraph of your article? It sets up a clear contrast between the old and new methods, and it creates reader interest.

Author:
Since this is going to be a short news article, these headings seem unnecessary.

(run in)

Figure 3.5. Editing a news publication for clarity.

A News Publication

This sample is a brief article from the newsletter of a professional association (see Figure 3.5).

Verbal-Visual Orientation

1. *What does the writer perceive to be the verbal-visual orientation of the discourse?*
   The writer perceives the article as verbal-visual. Though exclusively verbal, it does incorporate headings to identify blocks of information.
2. *Is this orientation appropriate?*
   The writer has appropriately identified this news article as verbal-visual (see Figure 3.6). Because the discourse access is sequential, however, subheadings prove unnecessary. It is the persuasive aim of the discourse that solicits visual information: a picture of the subject might do the job.

Principles and Diagrams of Organization

1. *What is the principle of organization?*
   The news article has a hierarchical-categorical organization. Of primary importance is the overview of the production change: here the basic information is given and the subordinate persuasive aim satisfied. Of secondary importance is the specific description of the new system (with separate paragraphs for hardware and software). Of least importance is the final paragraph with its general guidelines for submissions. In addition, within each category of information, various principles of organization prove operative:
   a) Paragraphs #1 and #2 display a complex chronological and categorical organization: the writer briefly traces the history of the change and anticipates its benefits, simultaneously comparing and contrasting the old and new systems. This is potentially disorienting because no single principle of organization guides the discussion. Reversing the two paragraphs might serve to emphasize the categorical comparison/contrast.
   b) In paragraphs #3 and #4, the organization is strictly categorical between and within the paragraphs. The individual paragraphs for hardware and software seem unnecessary, especially because paragraph #3 is a single sentence.
   c) Paragraph #5 is chronological.
2. *How might the text be diagrammed?*
   If paragraph #2 is shifted to the beginning, this news article might be easily visualized as a funnel, with general information leading to specific information.

1. Discourse Aim   1   2   3   (4)   5
informative   persuasive/
                                            instructive

referential, but with obviously persuasive subordinate aim

2. Discourse Urgency   (1)   2   3   4   5
no immediate   immediate
attention   attention
required   required

appearing in professional association's newsletter, published semi-annually; info requires no immediate change in reader's procedures

3. Discourse Access   (1)   2   3   4   5
sequential   random

article is brief and reader will likely move through it once from start to finish; no need for later reference or info retrieval

4. Reader's Motivation   1   (2)   3   4   5
motivated   unmotivated

probably, because subject is pertinent to reader's field, assuming active professional interested in submitting articles to the association's journal

5. Reader's Education   (1)   2   3   4   5
educated: uneducated:
> 16 years   < 12 years
of school   of school
normally

6. Reader's Familiarity   1   2   (3)   4   5
with Subject   familiar   unfamiliar
a genuinely mixed readership here

7. Reader's Environment   1   2   (3)   4   5
no   numerous
distractions/   distractions/
interruptions   interruptions

office, but probably during a leisure period

Figure 3.6.   Verbal-visual orientation survey for the news publication.

Within the article, the opening and closing paragraphs mirror this funnel diagram, with a string-of-beads characterizing the middle paragraphs.

3. *Is this organization appropriate to the aim of the discourse? Does it serve to clarify the information?*

With paragraph #2 shifted to the beginning, the organization is appropriate: the opening paragraph summarizes the essential information and emphasizes the benefits of computerization, thereby satisfying the primary referential aim and subordinate persuasive aim. The remaining paragraphs add dimension.

4. *Is this organization appropriate to the audience of the discourse? Does it help readers to assimilate the information?*

The organization is appropriate for the audience. The members of this professional association might have a limited familiarity with this subject and its terminology. By grouping the information and establishing a hierarchy of importance, the writer gives the reader easier and quicker access to the information.

Coherence and Cohesion

1. *Does the writer establish a chain of given/new information? Is this chain achieved through repetition, substitution, or equivalence?*

The writer establishes a given/new ab–bc–cd chain of information, using repetition, substitution, and logical equivalence. The chain breaks with paragraph #2: the opening sentence is repetitious of paragraph #1, offering only given information. This opening sentence might therefore be easily omitted. If the entire paragraph is shifted to the beginning of the article, however, its general overview provides new information and leads appropriately to the specific information of the following sentences.

2. *Does the writer use sufficient and appropriate transitions?*

If paragraph #2 is shifted to the beginning, the transition *instead of* appropriately emphasizes the categorical comparison/contrast as a guiding principle of organization. Paragraphs #3 and #4 identify the equipment and briefly raise the issue of compatibility of different equipment: the single transition of *however* is here sufficient. The final paragraph, with its chronological organization, also displays appropriate transitions: *until* and *once*.

3. *Does the writer use parallel wording and phrasing as necessary?*

Parallel phrasing occurs as necessary (e.g., in the final paragraph, a series of "from" phrases).

4. *Does the writer use sufficient and appropriate headings? Are the coordinate and subordinate headings clearly and logically ordered?*

Because the discourse is brief and access sequential, subheadings seem unnecessary and distracting.

5. *Do the size, value, and position of headings clearly indicate their degree of importance?*
The single upper/lower case, plain, centered heading is sufficient to indicate the importance and unity of this article.

A Promotional Publication

This sample of a promotional publication is distributed by the Department of English, Texas A&M University (see Figure 3.7).

Verbal/Visual Orientation

1. *What does the writer perceive to be the verbal-visual orientation of the discourse?*
The writer seems to perceive this publication as verbally oriented: it is uninterrupted text.
2. *Is this orientation appropriate?*
The writer seems to be ignoring several important characteristics of this publication that give it a visual orientation (see Figure 3.8).

Principles and Diagrams of Organization

1. *What is the principle of organization?*
This promotional publication has a categorical organization. It identifies a problem (i.e., the growing demand for highly skilled writers) and offers a solution (i.e., the Writing Specialization). Within each category, a hierarchical organization is operative: the discussion progresses from the general to the specific.
2. *How might the text be diagrammed?*
The publication might be effectively diagrammed as a string-of-beads: the ordering of problem and solution might be easily reversed. Each of these two categories of information might be visualized as a funnel, if the opening two sentences of paragraph #1 are established as a new paragraph #2. The two sentences constitute a general description of the Writing Specialization and are thus appropriately grouped with the discussion of the solution to the problem identified in paragraph #1.
3. *Is this organization appropriate to the aim of the discourse? Does it serve to clarify the information?*
The problem-solution organization is appropriate to the persuasive aim of this promotional publication: first, a need is identified in broad terms and specific examples are given; then a means for satisfying this need is offered, again in broad terms, with the details following.

The Writing Specialization
Texas A&M University

(bf)

Author:
Should these first
two sentences be
moved to form the
2nd paragraph?
That way the 1st
paragraph states
the problem and
the 2nd offers the
solution.

¶

Author:
Since this is a
promotional piece,
I think you will
need to make it
visually attractive.
What kinds of illus-
trations might you
incorporate?

The Writing Specialization is a program designed to give students in business, scientific, technical, or humanistic disciplines eighteen hours of intensive training in a broad range of communication skills. Students who achieve a grade of B or better in all eighteen hours of coursework will receive a certificate signifying their successful completion of this training. ¶Because of the growing demand for highly skilled, professionally competent writers in business, industry, and government, the student with training in writing, speaking, editing, and communication skills has improved job opportunities. Often the individual who possesses such skills gets a job sooner and advances faster than someone without those skills. The biologist writing an environmental impact report, the computer specialist designing a user's manual for new software, or the acccountant explaining an auditing procedure to a client--every professional must be able to communicate ideas effectively and efficiently.

All students choosing this program will take four core courses: ¶English 210, Argumentation and Composition (the evaluation and composition of arguments through an intensive study of the logical processes of induction and deduction and the techniques of persuasion; ¶English 301, Technical Writing (writing proposals, memos, letters, and various types of business and technical reports for specialist and non-specialist audiences; ¶English 320, Technical Editing (study and practice of the rhetorical skills required of professional editors, from copyediting and proofreading to document design and desktop publishing; and Speech Communication 404, Technical and Professional Speaking (composing and delivering oral presentations of technical material using various media. In addition, the student will select six hours of supporting courses usually connected with the student's major. Students, in consultation with the

Figure 3.7. Editing a promotional publication for clarity.

(bf)

Writing Specialization Coordinator in the Department of
English, can thereby create their own program of special
emphasis.

To register for the The Writing Specialization or
to receive more information about it, contact Sam Dragga
(409-845-8304), 201D Blocker Building, Department of
English, Texas A&M University, College Station, TX 77843.

Figure 3.7. Editing a promotional publication for clarity (cont'd).

4. *Is this organization appropriate to the audience of the discourse? Does it
help readers to assimilate the information?*
The problem-solution organization is appropriate to the readers of this publication, especially given their limited motivation and their unfamiliarity
with this subject. This audience is unaware of both the problem and solution
to it: because the publication informs them of both, readers might consider
the problem compelling and this available solution desirable.

Coherence and Cohesion

1. *Does the writer establish a chain of given/new information? Is this chain
achieved through repetition, substitution, or equivalence?*
As is, the long opening paragraph displays a complicated and difficult given/
new chain of ab–bc–de. The third sentence thus breaks the chain of information, introducing only new information. As a consequence, the writer might
consider moving the initial two sentences of paragraph #1 and establishing
them as a new paragraph #2. Paragraph #1 would then have a given/new
chain of ab–bc–bd–be: using substitution, the writer offers the same given information in the second, third, and fourth sentences, thereby allowing the
reader to focus easily on the new information. Similarly, new paragraphs
#3 and #4 continue the simple given/new chain established in new para-
graph #2: ab–bc–bd–be–bf.
2. *Does the writer use sufficient and appropriate transitions?*
Because the given/new chain is simple, the associations among sentences
seem clear. The only explicit transition which does occur is *in addition*,
reinforcing the simple bc–bd–be–bf chain.
3. *Does the writer use parallel wording and phrasing as necessary?*
In the examples of professional writers and the identification of courses,
the writer appropriately uses parallel phrasing.

1. **Discourse Aim**   1   2   3   4   (5)

                   informative   persuasive/
                                                                instructive

document is designed to interest reader in the writing program

2. **Discourse Urgency**   1   2   (3)   4   5

                 no immediate   immediate
                 attention   attention
                 required   required

the sooner the reader decide to enroll, the better in order to allow enough time to complete course requirements

3. **Disourse Access**   1   2   3   (4)   5

                 sequential   random

reader will probably scan the document, jumping around in the text, skipping sections, reading quickly

4. **Reader's Motivation**   1   2   3   (4)   5

                 motivated   unmotivated

a mixed audience here, but given the typical negative attitude of people to writing, a document describing a writing program is probably not going to be enthusiastically received; but it does have to do with the reader's college and professional career and therefore might arouse at least curiosity

5. **Reader's Education**   1   2   (3)   4   5

                 educated: uneducated:
                 > 16 years   < 12 years
                 of school   of school

college students, normally during their second or third year

6. **Reader's Familiarity**   1   2   3   (4)   5
      with Subject   familiar   unfamiliar

reader will be generally familiar with writing course and may even have heard of this particular program, but the rationale and specific requirements will probably be new information

7. **Reader's Environment**   1   2   3   4   (5)

                 no   numerous
                 distractions/   distractions/
                 interruptions   interruptions

various: dormitory room, advisor's office, cafeteria, etc.

Figure 3.8.   Verbal-visual orientation survey for the promotional publication.

4. Does the writer use sufficient and appropriate headings? Are the coordinate and subordinate headings clearly and logically ordered?
Though subheadings seem unnecessary in this brief promotional publication, the courses might be displayed as a list to allow easier access to this information.

5. Do the size, value, and position of headings clearly indicate their degree of importance?
The upper/lower case, plain, centered heading dominates the publication. Because the opening paragraph of the publication never mentions the Writing Specialization, however, it might be effective to bold the words *The Writing Specialization* at the beginning of new paragraphs #2 and #4 to assist readers in locating information about the program. Bolding the title of the program as well as the course designations is sufficient to emphasize them without interfering with the superior importance of the heading.

REFERENCES

1. E. P. J. Corbett, *Classical Rhetoric for the Modern Student*, 2nd edition, Oxford University Press, New York, 1971.
2. N. A. Shearer, Alexander Bain and the Genesis of Paragraph Theory, *Quarterly Journal of Speech, 58*, pp. 408-417, 1972.
3. P. C. Rodgers, Jr., Alexander Bain and the Rise of the Organic Paragraph, *Quarterly Journal of Speech, 51*, pp. 399-408, 1965.
4. P. C. Rodgers, Jr., A Discourse-Centered Rhetoric of the Paragraph, *College Composition and Communication, 17*, pp. 2-11, 1966.
5. P. C. Rodgers, Jr., The Stadium of Discourse, *College Composition and Communication, 18*, pp. 178-185, 1967.
6. W. L. Pitkin, Discourse Blocs, *College Composition and Communication, 20*, pp. 138-148, 1969.
7. W. L. Pitkin, Hierarchies and the Discourse of Hierarchy, *College English, 38*, pp. 648-659, 1977.
8. B. F. and M. S. Barton, Toward a Rhetoric of Visuals for the Computer Era, *The Technical Writing Teacher, 12*, pp. 126-145, 1985.
9. S. Bernhardt, Seeing the Text, *College Composition and Communication, 35*, pp. 66-78, 1986.
10. P. J. Benson, Writing Visually: Design Considerations in Technical Publications, *Technical Communication, 32*, pp. 35-39, 1985.
11. J. Bertin, *Graphics and Graphic Information-Processing*, W. J. Berg and P. Scott (trans.), Walter de Gruyter and Co., Berlin, 1981.
12. H. R. Booher, Relative Comprehensibility of Pictorial Information and Printed Words in Procedural Instruction, *Human Factors, 17*, pp. 266-277, 1975.
13. G. Kaufmann, *Visual Imagery and its Relation to Problem Solving*, Universitetsforlaget, Bergen, Norway, 1979.

14. A. Paivio, *Imagery and Verbal Processes,* Holt, Rinehart, and Winston, New York, 1971.
15. M. L. and J. J. Koran, Jr., Interaction of Learner Characteristics with Pictorial Adjuncts in Learning from Science Text, *Journal of Research in Science Teaching, 17,* pp. 477–483, 1980.
16. G. Salomon, Internalization of Filmic Schematic Operations in Interaction with Learners' Aptitudes, *Journal of Educational Psychology, 66,* pp. 499–511, 1974.
17. F. M. Dwyer, *Strategies for Improving Visual Learning,* Learning Services, State College, PA, 1978.
18. D. Dowdey, Literary Sciences: A Rhetorical Analysis of an Essay Genre and Its Tradition, Dissertation U. of Wisconsin, 1984.
19. R. Quirk et al., *A Grammar of Contemporary English,* Longman, London, 1972.
20. H. H. Clark and S. E. Haviland, Comprehension and the Given-New Contract, in *Discourse Production and Comprehension,* R. O. Freedle (ed.), Ablex, Norward, NJ, pp. 1–40, 1977.

CHAPTER 4

Style

RHETORICAL THEORY OF STYLE

Following invention and arrangement is the rhetorical canon of style. This canon is particularly difficult to define because of widely differing attitudes among rhetoricians on the function of style in effective discourse. And this problem of definition has been with us since classical times.

For Aristotle, a discourse is effective because it is rational as opposed to emotive: it is the integrity of the evidence and the way it is organized that is persuasive. The effective speaker thus focuses the audience's attention on the logic of what is said as opposed to how it is said [1, pp. 598-599]. As soon as the audience begins to notice the language of the discourse—the speaker's manner of expression—the effectiveness of the discourse is diminished. Aristotle thus advocates a natural or invisible style which exhibits the characteristics of dignity and propriety [2, pp. 39-40; 3, p. 58]. This perception of style, however, differs from the rhetorical traditions preceding and following Aristotle, specifically the Greek tradition of the Sophists and the Roman tradition of Cicero.

To the Sophists, the power of rhetoric resides in a speaker's ability to impress an audience with embellished language. Style is thus the emotional ornamentation of discourse: the emphasis is on *pathos* as opposed to *logos*, emotion as opposed to logic [2, p. 40].

To the Roman philosopher Cicero, however, effective discourse depends on the speaker's knowledge of the subject and understanding of human experience. Giving equal weight to emotion and logic, he declares that rhetorical style operates at three levels, each with a distinctive purpose: the *high* style is designed to persuade (pathos and logos), the *middle* to entertain or delight (pathos), and the *low* to instruct (logos) [2, p. 43; 4, p. 137].

Building on this Ciceronian tradition, the Roman rhetorician Quintilian also declares the importance of the speaker's familiarity with a wide variety of subjects; he emphasizes, however, the significance of the speaker's being a morally motivated and ethical individual [5, p. 173]. Quintilian thus espouses a rhetoric that balances *logos, pathos*, and *ethos*. He also ascribes to the canons of rhetoric equal merit in the composition of discourse and considers education to include the teaching of grammar (i.e., word choice and sentence structure) and the teaching of rhetoric. Grammatical studies give pupils a basic understanding of the characteristics of "correct" discourse, and rhetorical studies equip them to compose "correct" discourse [1, pp. 601–602; 2, p. 41].

In the Middle Ages, Quintilian's linking of grammatical and rhetorical studies evolves; however, because style is a distinguishing trait of discourse as well as a stage in the composition of discourse, it quickly comes to dominate rhetorical considerations [1, p. 603]. Ultimately, rhetoric itself is perceived as synonymous with stylistic issues. And the rhetorical heritage of the Renaissance is essentially a variety of perspectives on style. A scientific orientation emerges, emphasizing a plain style. English philosopher and essayist Francis Bacon, for example, advocates short sentences, simple words, and little or no ornamentation: that is, the style of a discourse, he declares, must suit the subject matter and the audience, and a plain style appropriately echoes the precision and objectivity characteristic of the observations of scientists. In direct opposition to this scientific perspective is the aesthetic orientation of a heavily metaphorical and highly ornate style designed to excite and invigorate [2, p. 45].

The competition between rhetoricians of the grand style (i.e., elaboration and complexity) and rhetoricians of the plain style (i.e., brevity and simplicity) thus has ancient origins. It is also a competition without victors, chiefly because neither style is always appropriate. Situations occur which require a grand style. For example, while composing a formal invitation or a ceremonial speech, a writer might find it desirable to use poetic diction (e.g., *o'er, aft, 'twixt*), inverted sentence structure (e.g., "Greatness was ne'er the purpose sought by this woman so humble."), or variant spellings (e.g., *mediaeval* instead of *medieval*). On the other hand, distinct from ceremonial language yet similarly embellished is the official style, which Richard Lanham characterizes as

... an unreadable, voiceless, impersonal style; a style built on euphemism and various kinds of poetic diction; above all, a style with a formulaic structure, "is" plus a string of prepositional phrases before and after. [6, p. 81]

The following sentence illustrates Lanham's description:

The process for the selection and evaluation of department managers is to involve the widest and deepest employee participation and the fullest exchange of ideas between employees and executives consistent with the requirements for sound management, flexibility, and the maintenance of proper standards in the operation of the department.

The plain style version of this sentence is clearer:

> Employees will work with executives to select and evaluate department managers as long as this does not interfere with the operation of the department.

Neither, however, is the plain style always appropriate. Consider, for example this scenario: Your supervisor reviews your job performance and gives you a letter that states simply "You're fired." This plain style is direct and clear; however, its brevity is here inappropriate. Similarly, a wedding invitation with the inscription "Please come to the wedding . . ." announces a fairly informal or unconventional affair, as opposed to "The honour of your presence is requested on the joyous occasion of the marriage of . . ." which implies a traditional and formal wedding. Obviously, the propriety of either the plain style or the grand style depends on the harmonious correspondence of what is said, who says it, how it is said, to whom it is said, and when and where it is said. As Corbett explains:

> This notion of the integral relationship between matter and form is the basis for any true understanding of the rhetorical function of style. It precludes the view that style is merely the ornament of thought or that style is merely the vehicle for the expression of thought. Style does provide a vehicle for thought, and style can be ornamental; but style is something more than that. It is another of the "available means of persuasion," another of the means of arousing the appropriate emotional response in the audience, and another of the means of establishing the proper ethical image. [1, p. 415].

Following Corbett's advice, we avoid prescriptive ideas of style and choose a descriptive perspective. We perceive the question of style along a linguistic continuum between the polarities of the grand and plain styles, as a question of degree of appropriateness or inappropriateness as opposed to a question of either right or wrong.

In addition, though historically style is discussed as strictly a verbal issue, we consider visual style equally important. We recognize the diversity of written discourse as well as the technology which allows the easier and easier integration of the verbal and visual display of information. A critical editorial consideration is thus the propriety of various illustrations to a given rhetorical situation and the effect of illustrations on the rhetorical power of the discourse.

In this chapter on style, we will therefore consider 1) levels of discourse and the dimensions of verbal style, 2) kinds of illustrations and the dimensions of visual style, and 3) strategies of editing for propriety.

Verbal Style

Verbal style is a critical consideration on three distinct levels of a text or utterance; the *lexical* level (i.e., word choice); the *grammatical* level (i.e., sentence structure); and the *mechanical* level (i.e., spelling and punctuation). In addition, according to English linguists David Crystal and Derek Davy, there are eight dimensions or sources of style: *individuality, dialect, time, singularity, discourse medium and participation, province, status,* and *modality.* The subject of style is thus especially complex because the eight dimensions of style have a significant effect on all three levels of a text. To illustrate this complexity, we will define and exemplify how each dimension influences stylistic considerations on each level.

Individuality

This refers to personal and distinctive stylistic features which a writer or speaker introduces into a text or utterance, without realizing he or she is doing so [7, pp. 66-67]:

Lexical: a writer might prefer the expression *for instance* over *for example* or *e.g.* and always use the preferred expression without giving it thought.

Grammatical: a writer might habitually pair adjectives (e.g., "kind and considerate man" or "bright and perceptive woman") or might develop a habit of beginning sentences with participial phrases (e.g., "Writing the book without a typewriter, Bill never thought he would finish as quickly as he did.)

Mechanical: a writer might unintentionally and routinely number items in a series instead of alphabetizing or bulleting them.

Dialect

This refers to geographic or class characteristics which might distinguish writers or speakers of a language [7, p. 67].

Lexical: while the English ride on *lifts*, Americans ride on *elevators*, and while New Yorkers place their groceries in *bags*, Mississippians place theirs in *sacks.*

Grammatical: though the *s*-ending on possessive nouns (e.g., *Bill's book*) is typical and has prestige, dialects of English omit this ending (e.g., *Bill book*).

Mechanical: while the English go to the *theatre*, Americans go to the *theater*, and while the English might do you a *favour*, Americans do you a *favor.*

Time

This refers to temporal characteristics which might identify the period during which the discourse was composed and/or the age of the speaker/writer [7, pp. 67-68].

Lexical: while a writer in 1925 might refer to *moving pictures*, a writer in 1985 might refer to *motion pictures* or to *films* or to *movies*, never to *moving pictures*.

Grammatical: a writer in 1925 might distinguish between *shall* and *will*, using *shall* only with 1st person (e.g., "I shall") and *will* with 2nd or 3rd person (e.g., "you will" or "he will"); a writer in 1985 is likely to perceive *shall* and *will* as always interchangeable, with *shall* possibly considered archaic.

Mechanical: A writer in 1925 might spell *preëminent* with a dieresis (or pair of dots) above the second *e* to signal that the adjacent vowels symbolize two distinct sounds; a writer in 1985, however, typically spells *preeminent* without the dieresis.

Singularity

This refers to the conscious individual choices of the writer regarding wording, grammar, and mechanics. It is this dimension of style which is usually called the "author's style." It is here that the individual's originality or creativity is exhibited [7, pp. 76-77].

Lexical: A writer might choose to obscure ideas with multisyllabic words or clarify information using monosyllabic words (e.g., *criminalities* versus *crimes*).

Grammatical: A writer might like to compose sentences with long introductory phrases or clauses.

Mechanical: A writer might wish to avoid semicolons and link sentences using colons.

Discourse Medium and Participation

Medium refers to the stylistic features resulting from the spoken or written composition of the discourse: that is, utterance or text. Spoken discourse is usually vocalized and perceived within a single situation, and communication is thus aided through tacit signals (e.g., visual aids, vocal pitch and volume, hand motions, facial expressions). Written discourse, however, is perceived only as communication which has been previously composed, and thus all information must occur as words or illustrations within the discourse. The relationship between speaking and writing in a discourse, however, might be complex: a discourse composed orally might be subsequently written (e.g., a dictated memo), or a discourse might be composed in writing to imitate speaking (e.g., a scripted speech) [7, pp. 68-69]. And the style of a discourse intended to be *read* typically differs from the style of a discourse intended to be *heard*: that is, the graphic permanency of a written text makes it available for continuous review and analysis, and this allows a dense organization of ideas with minimal repetition.

Participation refers to the stylistic features resulting from the individual or reciprocal composition of the discourse: that is, monologue or dialogue. In monologue, a single communicator chooses the ideas, the words, the images which compose the discourse; in dialogue, no single communicator has a similar opportunity or obligation. Simple and complex manners of participation also occur: a discourse might be individually composed as though it were dialogue (as with the script of a drama) or a discourse might be composed through a collaborative and reciprocal process to imitate monologue (as with a jointly authored book) [7, pp. 69-71].

The medium and participation of discourse also typically co-occur: that is, spoken discourse is usually dialogue and written discourse is usually monologue. Because of this association, spoken discourse has a sociocentric orientation: that is, during composing, each speaker is also a visible or audible listener and is therefore sensitive to the needs of both speakers and listeners in the dialogue. Written discourse, however, has a decidedly egocentric orientation: that is, during composing, a single individual serves simultaneously as the only writer and reader of the monologue, and it is common for this writer/reader to perceive the discourse as a soliloquy and ignore or forget the needs of subsequent readers. (Collaborative composing and/or revising minimize the consequences of this orientation.)

Lexical: In spoken dialogue, miscellaneous voiced pauses and meaningless words (e.g., "Well, ..." or "..., okay?" or "... you know ...") serve as the speaker's way of keeping his or her speaking role in the reciprocal discourse: that is, the speaker continues to utter sounds while thinking of a meaningful message to deliver to the listener, who is waiting to assume the speaking role in order to deliver a meaningful message. In written monologue, with no exchange of roles occurring between the writer and the reader, such meaningless words prove unnecessary and distracting, unless the writer wishes to imitate conversation.

Grammatical: In spoken sentences using indefinite pronouns such as *everyone* or *nobody*, the plural personal pronoun is typically used to refer to them: "*Everyone* enrolled in the class brought *their* book." It is likely that at the point the personal pronoun is voiced, neither the speaker nor the listeners recognize that the subject earlier voiced was grammatically singular. In written sentences, however, the full sentence with its obviously singular subject (*-one, -body*) is visible to the writer and the reader and, as a consequence, singular personal pronouns refer to indefinite pronouns in written sentences: for example, "*Everyone* enrolled in the class brought *his or her* book."

Mechanical: Sounds compose the spoken language and miscellaneous graphic symbols compose the written language. In addition, spoken language has mechanical ways of imitating written language (e.g., a speaker beginning and ending a quotation with the words *quote* and *unquote*, respectively, as substitutes for the quotation marks of written language); similarly, written language has mechanical ways of imitating spoken language (e.g., variant spellings to imitate a speaker's pronunciation of words.)

Province

This refers to the characteristics of the discipline associated with the discourse [7, pp. 71-73].

Lexical: In the fields of music and construction, the meaning of the word *pitch* is quite different.

Grammatical: In the experimental sciences, the analysis of information is more important than who did the analyzing, and, as a consequence, scientists will often use passive voice. This grammatical structure emphasizes what happened as opposed to who or what was involved: for example, "The scores were analyzed [by the researcher] to determine their statistical significance." as opposed to "The researcher analyzed the scores to determine their statistical significance."

Mechanical: In documenting sources of information, different fields use different systems. For example, literary critics follow the system of the Modern Language Association (MLA), which asks for a parenthetical citation comprising the author's name and the page number on which the cited material occurs. Researchers in the field of management, however, adopt the system of the American Psychological Association (APA), which asks for a parenthetical citation comprising the author's name and the year of publication.

Status

This refers to the stylistic features resulting from the hierarchical relationship between the writer and reader: that is, superior, equal, or subordinate. The status continuum (superior-equal-subordinate) is associated with levels of formality/ informality [7, pp. 73-74]. For example, if the writer is the superior of the reader and wishes to emphasize this superiority, the writer will use formal language associated with power and prestige; to minimize this superiority, the writer will choose the informal language with which equals speak to equals. Similarly, if the writer is the subordinate of the reader and wishes to emphasize the reader's superiority, the writer will use formal language associated with polite subservience; if the writer wishes to minimize this superiority, the writer will choose the informal language of equals.

Lexical: *Yes* is typically perceived as formal, and *yeah* as informal.

Grammatical: In formal discourse, writers distinguish between *who* and *whom*, using *who* for the subject of a clause and using *whom* for the object of a clause (e.g., *"Who* came to the door?" versus *"Whom* did you see?"). Writers of informal discourse typically ignore this distinction, using *who* as either subject or object.

Mechanical: Contractions are typically considered appropriate for informal discourse; uncontracted forms are perceived as formal.

Modality

This refers to the distinctive characteristics of specific types of discourse: that is, a business letter, a user's manual, a research proposal, etc. [7, pp. 74-76].

Lexical: Only in a business letter does a writer address the reader as "Dear. . . ."

Grammatical: In a series of instructions, the writer gives the reader a series of commands (e.g., "Select the object you wish to measure. Position the pointer in the middle of the object."). With a quiz, the writer only asks questions of the reader (e.g., "What is the capital of Arizona?" or "Who is the governor of Connecticut?"). Similarly, while phrases and clauses might be appropriate to a resumé (e.g., "Developed editorial policies of company."), the accompanying letter of application ought to have full sentences (e.g., *"I* developed *the* editorial policies of *the* company.").

Mechanical: In a personal letter, the salutation has a comma following it (e.g., "Dear Bill,"); in a business letter, it has a colon following it (e.g., "Dear Ms. Cooper:").

Visual Style

Typically we associate the style of a text with its words; however, illustrations also determine style because different illustrations communicate different messages and achieve different effects within a text, as do different words or sentence structures or spellings.

There are basically two kinds of illustrations: *tables* and *figures*. This distinction is an important one for the editor to maintain for two reasons: 1) Tables and figures are numbered and listed separately in a text: that is, Table 1, Table 2, etc., and Figure 1, Figure 2, etc. A text which has only tables will have a List of Tables. A text which has only figures will have a List of Figures. And a text which has both tables and figures will have a List of Illustrations. 2) Tables are verbally oriented and thus must be read very much like a verbal text in order to be understood. Figures, on the other hand, are visually oriented, requiring not so much reading as seeing in order to be understood: that is, comprehension of a figure is possible following a simple scanning of the figure.

Table 4.1. The Verbal-Visual Orientation of Tables

	Verbal	*Visual*
Discourse aim	**Informative**	Persuasive/Instructive
Discourse urgency	**No immediate attention**	Immediate attention
Discourse access	Sequential	**Random**
Reader's motivation	**Motivated**	Unmotivated
Reader's Education	**Educated**	Uneducated
Reader's familiarity with subject	**Familiar**	Unfamiliar
Reader's environment	**No distractions/ interruptions**	Numerous distractions/interruptions

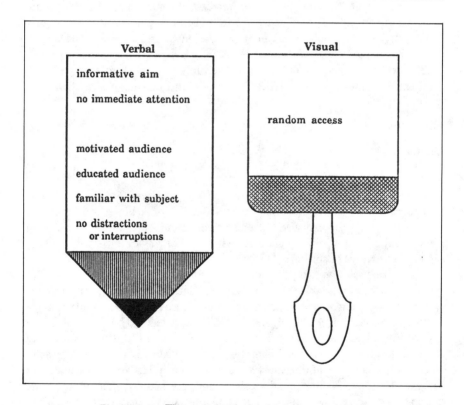

Figure 4.1. The verbal-visual orientation of tables.

Table 4.2. The Verbal-Visual Orientation of Figures

	Verbal	*Visual*
Discourse aim	Informative	**Persuasive/Instructive**
Discourse urgency	No immediate attention	**Immediate attention**
Discourse access	Sequential	**Random**
Reader's motivation	Motivated	**Unmotivated**
Reader's education	Educated	**Uneducated**
Reader's familiarity with subject	Familiar	**Unfamiliar**
Reader's environment	No distractions/ interruptions	**Numerous distractions/ interruptions**

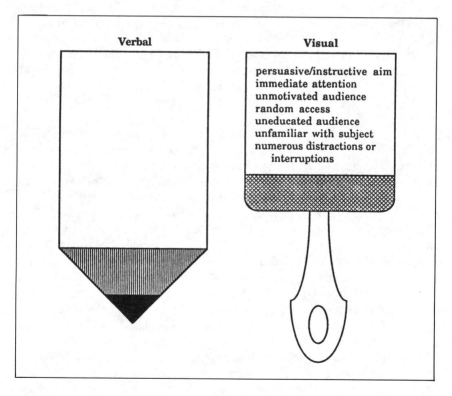

Figure 4.2. The verbal-visual orientation of figures.

Tables

Tables organize pieces of information (e.g., numerals, symbols, words) horizontally and vertically within a limited visual space in order to give readers random access to that information. Information which might be given in the sequential order of sentences and paragraphs is thus capsulized in columns and rows. The reader can choose which column or which row to read and can thus obtain desired information more rapidly than is possible by reading through an entire paragraph. The visual juxtaposition of categories of information also allows easier comparison and recollection of specific pieces of information. Tables are therefore not so much persuasive or instructive as they are simply informative: that is, giving readers access to objectively listed information.

Tables do, however, require a careful examination in order to be understood: that is, reading up and down the columns and across the rows. Access to the information is thus slower and more difficult than with other kinds of visuals. Tables, as a consequence, are better aimed at readers who do not have an urgent need for information, but who are fairly familiar with the subject matter, motivated, and educated. It is also easier to read a table in an environment without distractions and interruptions.

The above paragraphs might be capsulized as Table 4.1. The information in this table can also be visualized as Figure 4.1.

Figures

As the table and figure above illustrate, figures organize pieces of information visually, with a visual orientation as opposed to the verbal orientation of tables. In addition to giving readers random access to information as tables do, figures vivify and dramatize this information, making it more persuasive or instructive than a table, more demanding of immediate attention, more attractive to un-motivated or uneducated readers, and more understandable to readers unfamiliar with the subject or faced with distractions and interruptions of their reading process.

Again to illustrate the differing orientations of tables and figures, the charac-teristics of figures might be capsulized as Table 4.2. And the information in this table can also be visualized as Figure 4.2.

While all tables look essentially alike, organizing their information in columns and rows, figures come in a wide variety. Some kinds (e.g., drawings and photo-graphs), are more visually oriented than are other kinds (e.g., graphs and charts). And the labeling of the different kinds of figures is typically erratic. For ex-ample, while many *graphs* show change over time, some *charts* do also. But not all charts show change over time; several show the condition of a subject at a particular point in time. Often the labeling is interchangeable: for example,

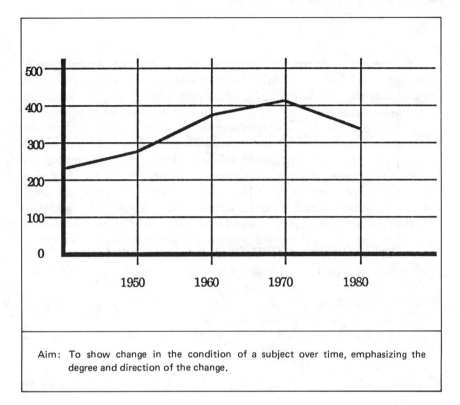

Aim: To show change in the condition of a subject over time, emphasizing the degree and direction of the change.

Figure 4.3. Line graph.

bar chart or *bar graph*. The following (Figures 4.3–4.14), therefore, is only a partial listing of the multitude of radically differing figures, with their various labels and common uses identified.

Similar to verbal style, visual style also has eight dimensions or sources.

Individuality

A writer might always and without deliberation choose bar charts over column charts.

Dialect

While Bostonians might without deliberation rely on drawings and photographs of Boston for illustrations of city life, Houstonians might also be likely to look to their surroundings and thus develop a different portrait of the subject.

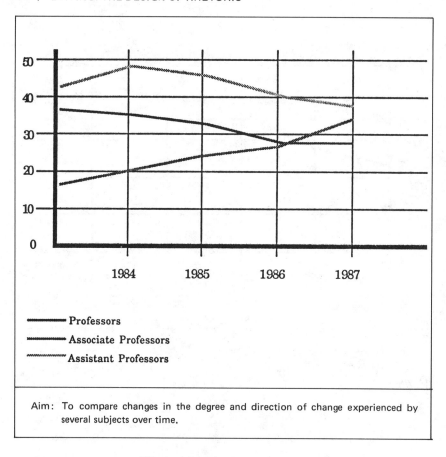

Figure 4.4. Multiple line graph.

Time

While fifty years ago photographs were restricted to professionally published texts because of the limitations of technology and the corresponding cost, photographs in 1985 might be easily and inexpensively incorporated into a wide variety of documents published in-house with a computer, optical scanning device, and laser printer.

Singularity

As a conscious and deliberate choice, a writer might always avoid multiple line graphs, rationally or irrationally perceiving them as hideous and unclear.

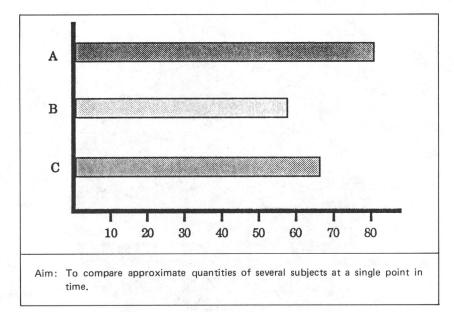

Figure 4.5. Bar chart.

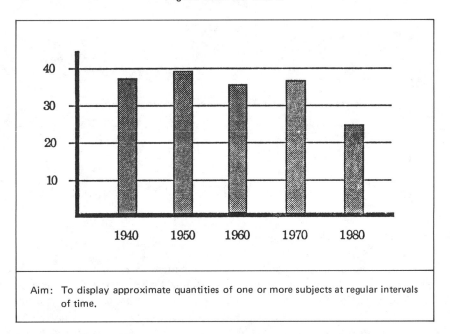

Figure 4.6. Column chart.

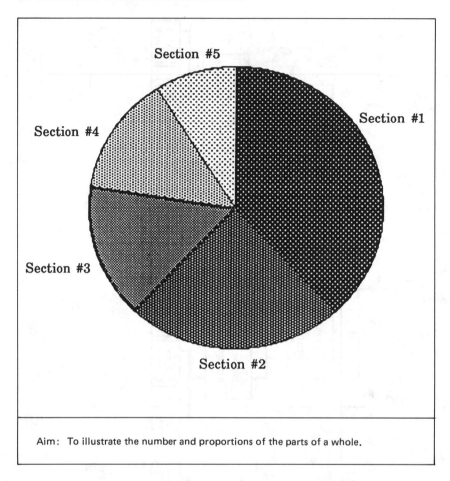

Aim: To illustrate the number and proportions of the parts of a whole.

Figure 4.7. Pie chart.

Discourse Medium and Participation

A writer might appropriately place information in a table for readers to examine thoroughly and according to their individual desires. A speaker might wish to expedite the audience's acquisition of information because of the temporal constraints of the oral presentation, and might thus emphasize only pertinent information by placing it in a quickly and easily perceived figure.

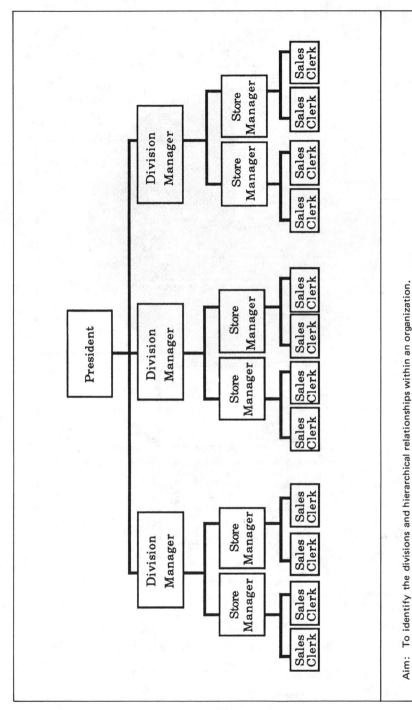

Aim: To identify the divisions and hierarchical relationships within an organization.

Figure 4.8. Organizational chart.

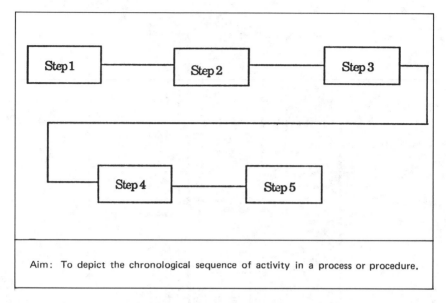

Aim: To depict the chronological sequence of activity in a process or procedure.

Figure 4.9. Flow chart.

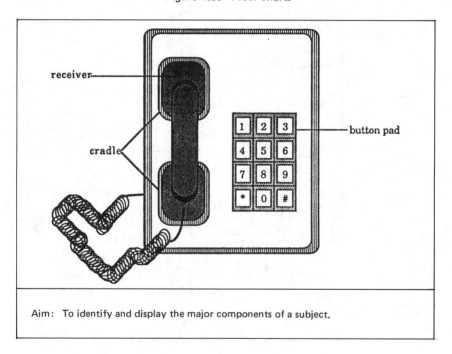

Aim: To identify and display the major components of a subject.

Figure 4.10. Diagram.

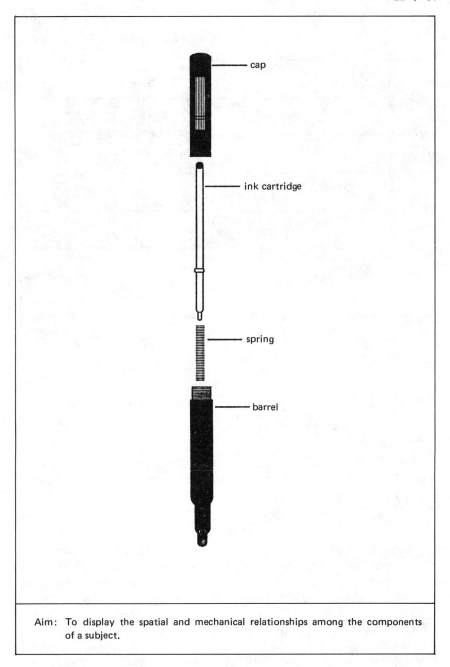

cap

ink cartridge

spring

barrel

Aim: To display the spatial and mechanical relationships among the components of a subject.

Figure 4.11. Exploded diagram.

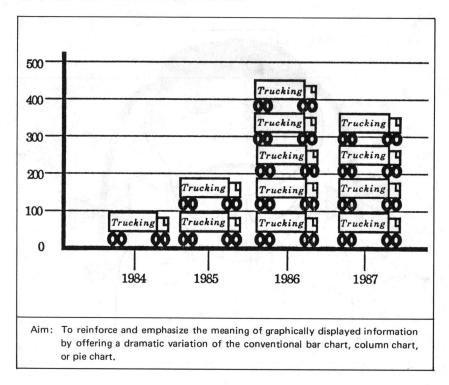

Figure 4.12.   Pictograph.

Province

Different visuals characterize the texts of different disciplines: for example, engineering typically incorporates diagrams, accounting has numerous tables, and marketing uses charts and graphs.

Status

Illustrations might be hierarchically organized according to the technological sophistication, complexity, and cost associated with their composition: that is, the occurrence of photographs in a text is typically perceived as impressive, drawings and diagrams less impressive, charts and graphs again less impressive, and tables fairly unimpressive. Conversely, illustrations might also be hierarchically organized according to their verbal or visual orientation: that is, a visually oriented illustration such as a photograph is perceived as bringing informality to a text and a verbally oriented illustration such as a table is perceived as bringing formality to a text. Thus a technologically sophisticated and visually oriented

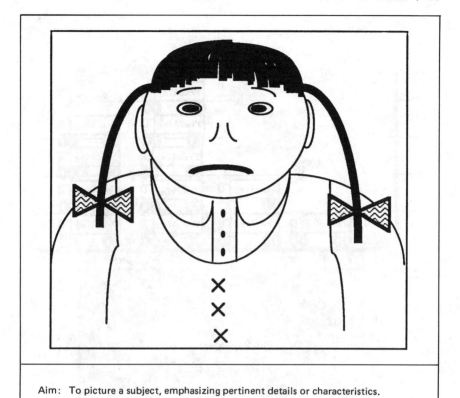

Aim: To picture a subject, emphasizing pertinent details or characteristics.

Figure 4.13. Drawing.

illustration is perceived as impressive, though informal. The appropriate balance between impressive/unimpressive and formal/informal must be determined according to the relationship between the writer and reader (i.e., superior, equal, subordinate). An impressive/informal illustration would thus be effectively used only by 1) equals communicating with equals; 2) superiors communicating to subordinates if the superiors wish to minimize their superiority and persuade or please the subordinates; and 3) subordinates communicating with superiors if the subordinates wish to minimize their subordination and maximize their authority. In this third case, there is a significant risk of the subordinate being perceived as impertinent, and thus it might be important for subordinates addressing their superiors either to choose less impressive and more formal illustrations or to insure that their verbal style compensates through its formality for the informality of their visual style.

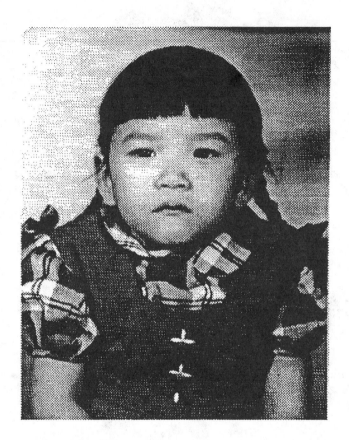

Aim: To picture a subject as realistically as possible, emphasizing actual appearance.

Figure 4.14. Photograph.

Modality

Different visuals also characterize different kinds of texts: for example, user's manuals depend on numerous diagrams, while annual reports ordinarily contain tables, charts, graphs, drawings, and photographs.

Editing for Propriety

Because editing for propriety often involves making scores of important and unimportant style decisions, the editor typically starts by composing a style guide: that is, a listing of the style issues associated with the discourse. Initially, this style guide is a blank series of alphabetical and miscellaneous categories (see Figure 4.15). Ultimately, it is a record of the editor's decisions and thus helps the editor to be as consistent and careful as possible in the application of his or her style decisions. The discourse to be edited, however, might have to comply strictly with the dictates of a comprehensive style book (e.g., *Chicago Manual of Style*): in this situation, the majority of style issues have been decided, and the editor's job is to apply the decisions uniformly and rigorously to the discourse. Nevertheless, a style guide is still necessary, as a listing of reminders to the editor of the style book's guidelines on a given issue and as a listing of all dubious or ambiguous issues.

The typical editor also has basic style resources on hand; that is, books which might help the editor cautiously and meticulously evaluate the propriety of the verbal and visual characteristics of a given discourse. For example, the following bibliography covers *dictionaries*, which identify common and uncommon spellings and definitions; *style manuals*, which explain and illustrate systems of bibliographic citation and offer instruction on the formatting of texts; *grammars*, which register the conventions of sentence structure and punctuation; and *usage guides*, which give advice on writing and word choice.

Dictionaries

General

The American Heritage Dictionary, 2nd edition, Houghton Mifflin, Boston, 1982.
Webster's New Collegiate Dictionary, 9th edition, Merriam, Springfield, Massachusetts, 1983.
Webster's New World Dictionary of the American Language, 2nd edition, Simon & Schuster, New York, 1982.

Special

Bartlett, J., *Bartlett's Familiar Quotations*, 15th edition, Little Brown, Boston, 1980.

A	
B	
C	
D	
E	
F	
G	
H	
I	
J	
K	
L	
M	
N	
O	
P	
Q	
R	
S	
T	
U	
V	
W	
X,Y,Z	
1,2,3	

Figure 4.15. Blank style guide.

Black, H. C., *Black's Law Dictionary*, 5th edition, West Publishing, St. Paul, 1979.

Brandon, S. G. F. (ed.), *A Dictionary of Comparative Religion*, Scribner, New York, 1970.

Campbell, R. J., *Psychiatric Dictionary*, 5th edition, Oxford University Press, New York, 1981.

Connors, T. D. (ed.), *Longman's Dictionary of Mass Media and Communication*. Longman, New York, 1982.

Dorland's Illustrated Medical Dictionary, 26th edition, W. B. Saunders, Philadelphia, 1981.

Evans, I. H. (ed.), *Brewer's Dictionary of Phrase and Fable*, rev. edition, Cassell, London, 1981.

Hammond, N. G. and H. H. Scullard (eds.), *The Oxford Classical Dictionary*, 2nd edition, Oxford University Press, Oxford, 1970.

Harre, R., and R. Lamb (eds.), *The Encyclopedic Dictionary of Psychology*, MIT Press, Cambridge, 1983.

McGraw-Hill Dictionary of Scientific and Technical Terms, 3rd edition, McGraw-Hill, New York, 1984.

Mitchell, G. D. (ed.), *A New Dictionary of the Social Sciences*, 2nd edition, Aldine, Hawthorne, New York, 1979.

Nemmers, E. E., *Dictionary of Economics and Business*, 4th edition, Littlefield, Totowa, New Jersey, 1979.

Shapiro, I. J., *Dictionary of Marketing Terms*, 4th edition, Littlefield, Totowa, New Jersey, 1981.

Webster's Biographical Dictionary, rev. edition, Merriam, Springfield, Massachusetts, 1980.

Webster's New Geographical Dictionary, rev. edition, Merriam, Springfield, Massachusetts, 1984.

Style Manuals

General

American National Standard for Bibliographic References, American National Standards Institute, New York, 1977.

The Chicago Manual of Style, 13th edition, University of Chicago Press, Chicago, 1982.

Skillin, M. E., and R. M. Gay, *Words Into Type*, 3rd edition, Prentice-Hall, Englewood Cliffs, New Jersey, 1974.

U.S. Government Printing Office Style Manual, rev. edition, Government Printing Office, Washington, D.C., 1984.

Special

Agriculture and Agronomy

Handbook and Style Manual for ASA, CCSA and SSSA Publications, 6th edition, American Society of Agronomy, Madison, Wisconsin, 1984.

Biology

CBE Style Manual: A Guide for Authors, Editors, and Publishers in the Biological Sciences, 5th edition, Council of Biology Editors, Bethesda, Maryland, 1983.

Chemistry

Handbook for Authors of Papers in American Chemical Society Publications, American Chemical Society, Washington, D.C., 1978.

Handbook for AOAC Members, 5th edition, Association of Official Analytical Chemists, Washington, D.C., 1982.

Geology

Cochran, W., P. Fenner, and M. Hill (eds.), *Geowriting: A Guide to Writing, Editing, and Printing in Earth Science*, 3rd edition, American Geological Institute, Alexandria, Virginia, 1979.

Journalism

French, C. W., E. A. Powell, and H. Angione (eds.), *Associated Press Stylebook and Libel Manual*, Addison Wesley, Reading, Massachusetts, 1982.

Holley, F. S., *Los Angeles Times Stylebook: A Manual for Writers, Editors, Journalists and Students*, New American Library, New York, 1981.

Jordan, L., *The New York Times Manual of Style and Usage*, Times Books, New York, 1976.

Language and Literature

Achtert, W. S., and J. Gibaldi, *The MLA Style Manual*, Modern Language Association, New York, 1985.

Gibaldi, J., and W. S. Achtert, *The MLA Handbook for Writers of Research Papers*, 3rd edition, Modern Language Association, New York, 1988.

Law

A Uniform System of Citation, 13th edition, The Harvard Law Review Association, Cambridge, Massachusetts, 1981.

Linguistics

Linguistic Society of America, LSA Style Sheet, in *LSA Bulletin*, December issue, annually.

Mathematics

A Manual for Authors of Mathematical Papers, 7th edition, American Mathematical Society, Providence, Rhode Island, 1980.

Medicine

Barclay, W. R., M. T. Southgate, and R. W. Mayo, *Manual for Authors and Editors; Editorial Style and Manuscript Preparation*, 7th edition, Lange Medical Publications, Los Altos, California, 1981.

International Steering Committee of Medical Editors, Uniform Requirements for Manuscripts Submitted to Biomedical Journals, in *Annals of Internal Medicine, 90*, pp. 95-99, 1979.

Style Manual: Physical Therapy, 5th edition, American Physical Therapy Association, Washington, D.C., 1985.

Physics

Style Manual for Guidance in the Preparation of Papers, 3rd edition, American Institute of Physics, New York, 1978.

Psychology

Publication Manual of the American Psychological Association, 3rd edition, American Psychological Association, Washington, D.C., 1983.

Science

American National Standard for the Preparation of Scientific Papers for Written or Oral Presentation, American National Standards Institute, New York, 1979.

Social Work

Information for Authors about NASW Publications, National Association of Social Workers, Silver Spring, Maryland, 1985.

Grammars

Gefvert, C. J., *The Confident Writer*, 2nd edition, Norton, New York, 1988.

Hodges, J. C., and M. E. Whitten, *Harbrace College Handbook*, 10th edition, Harcourt Brace Jovanovich, New York, 1986.

Quirk, R., S. Greenbaum, G. Leech, and J. Svartvik, *A Grammar of Contemporary English*, Longman, London, 1972.

Quirk, R., S. Greenbaum, G. Leech, and J. Svartvik, *A Comprehensive Grammar of the English Language*, Longman, London, 1987.

Usage Guides

Cook, C. K., *The MLA's Line by Line: How to Edit Your Own Writing*, Houghton Mifflin, Boston, 1985.

Copperud, R. H., *American Usage and Style: The Consensus*, Van Nostrand Reinhold, New York, 1980.

Flesch, R., *The Art of Readable Writing*, 25th anniversary edition, Harper & Row, New York, 1974.

International Association of Business Communicators, *Without Bias: A Guidebook for Nondiscriminatory Communication*, 2nd edition, Wiley, New York, 1982.

Lanham, R. A., *Revising Business Prose*, Scribner, New York, 1981.

Miller, C., and K. Swift, *The Handbook of Nonsexist Writing*, Lippincott & Crowell, New York, 1980.

Rodale, J. I. (ed.), *The Synonym Finder*, rev. edition, Rodale Press, Emmaus, Pennsylvania, 1978.

Roget, P. M., *Roget's International Thesaurus*, 4th edition, Crowell, New York, 1977.

Strunk, W., Jr., and E. B. White, *The Elements of Style*, 3rd edition, Macmillan, New York, 1979.

Williams, J. M., *Style: Ten Lessons in Clarity and Grace*, 2nd edition, Scott Foresman, Glenview, Illinois, 1985.

Zinsser, W., *On Writing Well: An Informal Guide to Writing Nonfiction*, 2nd edition, Harper & Row, New York, 1980.

With a style guide and the necessary resources available, the editor analyzes the dominant dimensions of verbal style, the dominant dimensions of visual style, and thus the propriety of the verbal and visual styles.

Assessing the Propriety of the Verbal Style

The eight dimensions of style operating on the three levels of a text compose a verbal style matrix (see Figure 4.16) with which the editor might judge issues of propriety, using the style guide to register necessary decisions. The matrix capsulizes the responsibilities of the editor and his or her relationship with the author on matters of verbal style: that is, the editor's job is to insure that the style characteristics resulting from *individuality, dialect, time*, and *singularity* comply with the style guidelines of the *discourse medium and participation, province, status*, and *modality*. What the editor must never do is to impose his or her individuality or singularity on the discourse: to do so is to appropriate the text [8, p. 150], to make it the editor's text instead of the author's: that is, the editor's every style modification has as its only justification that it is appropriate to the discourse medium and participation, the modality, the status, and/or the province of the text.

The style matrix thus allows the editor to identify the possible sources of a problematic style trait as well as the level of text on which that trait occurs; given this identification, the editor might be better able to evaluate the appropriateness of that verbal characteristic to the text. For example, editors typically avoid direct address of the reader as "you," unless it is possible to attribute this style trait to the dimension of modality (e.g., a user's manual) or status (e.g., an

	Lexical	Grammatical	Mechanical
Individuality			
Dialect			
Time			
Singularity			
Discourse Medium and Participation			
Province			
Status			
Modality			

Figure 4.16. Verbal style matrix.

	Tables	Figures (nonpictorial-pictorial)
Individuality		
Dialect		
Time		
Singularity		
Discourse Medium and Participation		
Province		
Status		
Modality		

Figure 4.17. Visual style matrix.

informal memo to a subordinate). Recognition that this style trait operates on the grammatical level of the text also indicates the kind of editorial modification that might be necessary: that is, a re-phrasing (as opposed to a simple re-wording or re-spelling) with the deletion of *you*, the insertion of a singular third person reference (e.g., *one*), and possibly a change of verb ending to agree with the third person reference.

Assessing the Propriety of the Visual Style

Similarly, the editor must assess the visual style of the text, using the Visual Style Matrix (see Figure 4.17) to judge propriety and using the style guide to register decisions. Again, the editor's job is to insure that the style features resulting from the dimensions of *individuality, dialect, time,* and *singularity* comply with the style guidelines of the *discourse medium and participation, province, status,* and *modality*. The editor must avoid imposing his or her individuality or singularity on the discourse; instead, he or she must justify every style modification as appropriate to the discourse medium and participation, the modality, the status, and/or the province of the text. Using the style matrix, the editor can identify the possible sources of a problematic illustration as well as the kind of illustration that is problematic: with this information, the editor is better equipped to judge the appropriateness of that illustration to the text. For example, editors might avoid pictographs unless the dimension of status signals that a novel and informal display of information is necessary. In addition, the identification of the pictograph as a figure serves as a reminder that the pictograph heightens the visual orientation of the discourse. If this visual orientation is to be maintained without the pictograph, a different figure must be substituted (e.g., a traditional line graph or bar graph); substituting a table would heighten the formality of the discourse, but would also lessen its visual orientation.

PRACTICE

As has been seen, style is a complex subject, comprising a verbal display of eight dimensions occurring on three levels of a discourse as well as a visual display of eight dimensions occurring as tables or figures. In editing for propriety, as a consequence, different editors have different starting points and give different emphasis to the different levels of discourse and the different dimensions of style. For example, some editors typically focus on the lexical level of the verbal text, others emphasize the mechanical or grammatical levels, and still others exhibit a sensitivity to dialect or questions of formality and informality. This "style" of editing develops with experience, and every editor has a unique approach to the process of editing, especially editing for propriety.

Verbal Propriety
1. What are the verbal style characteristics of discourse medium and participation, province, status, and modality?
2. What are the verbal style characteristics of individuality, dialect, time, and singularity?
3. Do the verbal style characteristics of discourse medium and participation, province, status, and modality dominate the verbal style characteristics of individuality, dialect, time, and singularity?
4. Is the verbal style consistent across the lexical, grammatical, and mechanical levels of the discourse?

Visual Propriety
1. What are the visual style characteristics of discourse medium and participation, province, status, and modality?
2. What are the visual style characteristics of individuality, dialect, time, and singularity?
3. Do the visual style characteristics of discourse medium and participation, province, status, and modality dominate the visual style characteristics of individuality, dialect, time, and singularity?
4. Is the visual style consistent across the illustrations of the discourse?

Figure 4.18.   Editor's style inventory.

The following series of questions, the Editor's Style Inventory (see Figure 4.18), is thus designed to serve as a flexible guide to the process and allows the editor to analyze the verbal and visual style of technical publications, news publications, and promotional publications. With this inventory, the editor can identify stylistic improprieties and determine the necessary revisions. Using author queries, the editor can then recommend that the writer modify the verbal or visual style of the text. Or the editor can use paired editing symbols to change the style of the discourse directly (see Table 4.3).

In the following samples of technical, news, and promotional publications, we will illustrate the application of the Editor's Style Inventory.

Table 4.3. Editing Symbols for Propriety

in the text	in the margin	explanation
ca⌃not	⌣	close up
judgᵍment	⍦	delete and close up
word⸜processing	#	insert space
theatre	tr	transpose
etc.	sp	spell out
in the book⊙	⊙	insert period
However⸲ the majority	⌃	insert comma
of the following⊙	⊙	insert colon
without⸲therefore the	⌃	insert semi-colon
colleagues˅	˅	insert apostrophe
is the question.˅	˅	insert quotation marks
⸦e.g., teachers⸧	⸦ / ⸧	insert parentheses
⸦emphasis mine⸧	⸦ / ⸧	insert brackets
company⸗sanctioned	/ = /	insert hyphen
H₂O	∧	subscript
x²	∨	superscript

Evaluation page 15

RESULTS AND DISCUSSION

Writing Apprehension

Table One presents the results of the two two-
tailed t-tests for the changes in response to the Daly-
Miller Writing Apprehension Test (1975) across the
semester.

[Insert Table One here]

Curiously, students in both the control and the experimental groups showed significant increases in apprehension across the semester (t=2.21, t=2.16, p<.05). The
small but significant increases in apprehension were
clearly not expected, and, perhaps equally important,
did not distinguish between the control and experimental
group.

To test for the possibility that the Daly-Miller,
as a whole, was not sensitive enough to pick up differences in students' attitudes toward evaluation of their
writing, a subscale of ten items was created from that
test. These ten items—1, 2, 4, 6, 12, 18, 22, and 25—
all probe students' attitudes about having others read
their writing and about having their essays evaluated.
Table Two presents the results.

[Insert Table Two here]

Although the control group did not show significant
decreases on these ten items (t=0.86, p>.05), the experimental group improved significantly (t=2.68, p<.01).
Student writers in the experimental group responded positively to the one-to-one conferences in which they discussed their writing and suggestions for guided revision
with their instructors. In addition, these student writers became more
comfortable and confident about the evaluation process
in the experimental group when their essays were rated
the same by two outside readers. The rater agreement
and guidelines for revision seemed to put these student

Figure 4.19. Editing a technical publication for propriety.

Evaluation   page 16

writers at more ease about writing for other readers and *submitting*
~~turning in~~ essays for evaluation.

Two interesting questions emerge *from* ~~by considering~~ the
subscale results where students' overall apprehension
increased but their apprehension about evaluation de-
creased: Is writing apprehension ~~a single monolithic~~ *as influential and important an*
entity *as* ~~that~~ the Daly-Miller assumes it is? And how sen-
sitive is this test as an indicator of apprehension?

Writing Quality

Two different procedures were used for determining
writing quality in the ② groups. Control group essays
were graded in the traditional manner (A, B, C, etc.);
experimental group essays were ~~simultaneously~~ evaluated
holistically on a 0-100 scale. This difference coupled
with the fact that different topics for the expressive,
referential, and persuasive essays were used to measure
pre- and post-course writing quality make it impossible
to compare the two groups directly. *Nevertheless,* ~~I~~mprovement over the
semester can be at least estimated by comparing grades on
an early and later paper for the control group and by
comparing holistic scores of an early and a later paper
for the experimental group, ~~nevertheless~~.

In the first case, the results seemed valid in
light of the fact that the instructors' grades were
purely dependent on the perceived quality of the writing
(that is) not influenced by pedagogical considerations)
and the writing tasks chosen from the beginning and end
of the semester made roughly the same demands on the
student writers. In the second case, the results seemed
valid in light of the fact that the raters evaluated the
pre- and post-essays on the same scale and the writing
tasks were equivalent.

Table (Three) shows an estimate of the improvement in
writing quality over the semester based on the comparison
of early and later papers described above. Given the
~~results~~ *of the results* validity, the data suggest that both groups
improved significantly in writing quality ~~over the semester~~.

Figure 4.19. Editing a technical publication for propriety (cont'd).

Evaluation   page 17

[Insert Table Three here]

The control group showed some increase in writing quality
from the expressive essay to the persuasive essay (t= -
0.42, p<.01). However, the experimental group made
extraordinary progress from essay 1 to essay 5 (t=3.01,
p<.01). Again, ~~while~~ *though* the grades of students whose work
had been evaluated traditionally steadily increased,
their progress was not ~~near~~ *commensurate with* the increase in quality *of those* ~~that~~
students whose writing had been evaluated both by summa-
tive and formative techniques. The guided revision and
one-to-one conferencing seemed to (significantly) increase
the writing abilities of students.

To measure the reliability of raters of the experimental group's essays, a Spearman's Rho (i.e., a type of
correlation between rank order data) was used. The correlation coefficients for each of the five essays were
determined (#1=.39; #2=.54; #3=.74; #4=.67; #5=.58) and
averaged. The average of the coefficients is .58, a fair
correlation. For, even as Diederich reports in his own
research, for example, a correlation such as .67 is "far
from satisfactory, but it is typical. . . . I have rarely
been able to boost the average correlation between pairs
of readers above .50, and other examiners tell me that
this is about whay they get" (*1974, p.* 33).

Figure 4.19. Editing a technical publication for propriety (cont'd).

Evaluation   page 18

①

Table One
Writing Apprehension Results (Daly-Miller)

	MEAN		t
	Pre	Post	
Control (N 52)	72.5	76.2	-2.21*
Experimental (N 103)	68.7	72.3	-2.16*

$^a n = 52$. $^b n = 103$.
*p<.05

②

Table Two
Writing Apprehension Sub-scale Results

	MEAN		t
	Pre	Post	
Control (N = 52)	32.3	31.9	0.86
Experimental (N = 103)	32.6	31.7	2.68*

$^a n = 52$. $^b n = 103$.
*p<.01

③

Table Three
Improvement in Writing Quality

	MEAN		t
	Pre	Post	
Control (N = 52)	78.3	78.7	-0.42*
Experimental (N = 103)	75.3	77.4	-3.01*

$^a n = 52$. $^b n = 103$.
*p<.01

Figure 4.19. Editing a technical publication for propriety (cont'd).

	Lexical	Grammatical	Mechanical
Individuality	uses *while* and *since* in their contrastive and causative senses		no spaces with = signs, often spells numbers, spells *that is*
Dialect	p. 16: "at more ease" p. 17: "not near"		
Time			
Singularity	p. 16: numbering: two this, two that, first case, second case		
Discourse medium and participation	initial or medial transitions, concise and varied wording	variety of sentences	
Province	APA style: *while* and *since* refer to time only		APA citations, numerals for most numbers, uses *i.e.* in ( ), spacing with =
Status	clear but erudite wording	no split infinitives, variety of sentences, no neuter possessives, no dangling phrases	
Modality	concise and objective wording		

Figure 4.20.   Verbal style matrix for the technical publication.

A	*although* for *while*
B	*because* for *since*
C	
D	
E	
F	
G	
H	
I	*(i.e.,)*
J	
K	
M	*M* for Mean
N	
O	
P	
Q	
R	
S	*submit* for *turn in*
T	*though* for *while*
U	
V	
W	
X,Y,Z	
1,2,3	Table 2; two groups

Source citations: (author, year) or author (year); for quotes (year, p. X)
spacing: x = x
possessives: for people, *'s* or *of the*; for objects, *of the*
notes: superscript letters for specific entry notes; notes end with period

Figure 4.21. Style guide for the technical publication.

	Tables	Figures *(nonpictorial-pictorial)*
Individuality	unconventional notations/abbreviations	
Dialect		
Time		
Singularity		
Discourse medium and participation		
Province	composition research normally follows APA	
Status	formal table for credibility with peers	
Modality	typical for data display in research report	

Figure 4.22. Visual style matrix for the technical publication.

A Technical Publication

This sample is excerpted from a research report intended for publication in a professional journal (see Figure 4.19).

Verbal Propriety

1. What are the verbal style characteristics of discourse medium and participation, province, status, and modality?
See Figure 4.20. In empirical composition research, the major journals require compliance with APA guidelines. In addition, because this is written

discourse addressed to colleagues, sentence structures ought to be clear and varied, using conservative and conventional wording. Objective wording typifies technical writing.

2. *What are the verbal style characteristics of individuality, dialect, time, and singularity?*
See Figure 4.20. This writer shows limited familiarity with the conventions of APA style, but effectively uses explicit numbering to signal organization. Evidence of dialect also occurs.

3. *Do the verbal style characteristics of discourse medium and participation, province, status, and modality dominate the verbal style characteristics of individuality, dialect, time, and singularity?*
Province dominates individuality: APA requires correction of the writer's a) use of *while* and *since* to refer to time, b) spelling of numbers, and c) absence of spacing with equal sign. Status dominates dialect: the writing is to colleagues as opposed to geographical neighbors. Singularity, however, is appropriate: the writer's habit of numbering to signal organization accords with the guidelines of the dominant dimensions.

4. *Is the verbal style consistent across the lexical, grammatical, and mechanical levels of the discourse?*
Given the decisions registered in the style guide (see Figure 4.21), the verbal style of this discourse is consistent across all levels of the discourse.

Visual Propriety

1. *What are the visual style characteristics of discourse medium and participation, province, status, and modality?*
(See Figure 4.22). In empirical research reports, writers ordinarily communicate their statistical findings through formal tables, and this is likely to be the expectation of the academic professionals reading this discourse. In addition, the major research journals comply with APA guidelines on appropriate notations and abbreviations.

2. *What are the visual style characteristics of individuality, dialect, time, and singularity?*
See Figure 4.22. This writer shows limited familiarity with the conventions of APA style.

3. *Do the visual style characteristics of discourse medium and participation, province, status, and modality dominate the visual style characteristics of individuality, dialect, time, and singularity?*
Province dominates individuality: APA requires correction of the writer's notations and abbreviations in the three tables. Status also dominates individuality: compliance with conventional guidelines also enhances the writer's credibility with colleagues.

Author:
I think this label headline should be changed to a sentence headline in order to make the story sound more dynamic.

Texas Liberal Review Converts to Desktop Publishing
~~Electronic Publishing and Texas Liberal Review~~

(Texas Liberal Review)

Continuity will mark upcoming issues of the (TLRev),
even as we move away from old-fashioned typesetting to
desktop publishing in producing the journal. If all
goes as planned, the Spring 1988 issue will match the
style, format, and quality of earlier issues while ~~at the
same time~~ being produced by radically different means.
Instead of having the Texas State Printing Center typeset
articles for the Texas Liberal Review, we plan ~~now that
word processors are so widely used~~ to capture authors'
keystrokes whenever possible. With funds from both (TALCI)
and Texas State University, we have purchased equipment

(Texas Association for Liberal Critical Inquiry)

that should allow us to produce galley proofs ~~of TLRev~~ in
the editorial office without having to pay for typesetting services. The savings should be substantial, allowing TALCI to recoup its investment in less than a year.

For those interested in a detailed description of
the equipment ("robot talk" as one of our colleagues
calls it), we have a Compaq Deskpro 286 computer (with a
30 megabyte hard drive and a 5-1/4 inch floppy disk
drive), an Apple LaserWriter Plus printer, a full-page
portrait monitor, and a Microsoft serial mouse. The
software for our system runs on the MS-DOS Version 3
operating system. We will be using WordPositor word
processing software in conjunction with the PositivePublisher page layout software. Those authors who create

Figure 4.23.   Editing a news publication for propriety.

electronic manuscripts processed in WordPositor (MS-DOS,

5-1/4 inch floppy) will produce material most compatible

with our system; however, we should be able to accomo-

date any document converted to a DOS/ASCII file.

More information will be supplied at a later date

as we learn about our abilities (and inabilities) to

convert files from various word processing programs, from

different operating systems, and from several sizes of

microcomputer disks. *for now* Until further notice, all authors—

those who work at typewriters and those who work at word

processors—should continue to submit two paper ("hard")

copies of manuscripts for evalution by readers. Once an

article is accepted, we will request a disk from the

author if the work was prepared on a word processor.

Figure 4.23. Editing a news publication for propriety (cont'd).

4. Is the visual style consistent across the illustrations of the discourse?
According to the decisions registered in the style guide (see again Figure 4.21), the visual style is consistent across the illustrations of the discourse.

A News Publication

This sample is a brief article from the newsletter of a professional association (see Figure 4.23).

Verbal Propriety

1. What are the verbal style characteristics of discourse medium and participation, province, status, and modality?

	Lexical	Grammatical	Mechanical
Individuality			hyphenates *desk-top*, spells *discs*
Dialect			
Time			
Singularity	likes acronyms *TLRev*, TALCI		numerals for dates, brand names, and measures
Discourse medium and participation	minimal redundancy, concise wording	variety of sentences	
Province			spelling of *desktop, disks*
Status	spelling out acronyms for formality		
Modality	sentence heading instead of label, concise wording		

Figure 4.24. Verbal style matrix for the news publication.

A	
B	
C	
D	desktop; disks
E	
F	
G	
H	
I	
J	
K	
L	
M	
N	
O	
P	
Q	
R	
S	
T	spell out *TL Rev* always; spell out TALCI on first use only
U	
V	
W	
X,Y,Z	
1,2,3	two copies, 30 megabyte, 5 1/4 inch, Version 3, 1988

no visuals unless dynamic and informative

Figure 4.25. Style guide for the news publication.

	Tables	Figures (nonpictorial-pictorial)
Individuality		
Dialect		
Time		
Singularity		consider photo of equipment in use static, silly, and uninformative
Discourse Medium and Participation		
Province		
Status		photo for impressiveness
Modality		photo of equipment in use, if available and worthwhile

Figure 4.26.   Visual style matrix for the news publication.

See Figure 4.24. In a written communication of news, writers typically strive to eliminate verbosity and redundancy. Formality is necessary to establish the writer's credibility: as a consequence, writers preserve full names and titles, avoiding abbreviations. It is also important that a news article exhibit the conventions of the discipline (e.g., terminology and spellings) and be interesting or intriguing.

2. *What are the verbal style characteristics of individuality, dialect, time, and singularity?*
See Figure 4.24. This writer is basically familiar with the conventional spellings of technical terminology and uses the acronyms of the association exclusively.

3. *Do the verbal style characteristics of discourse medium and participation, province, status, and modality dominate the verbal style characteristics of individuality, dialect, time, and singularity?*
Province dominates individuality: the conventions of the discipline recommend correction of the writer's spellings of *desk-top* and *discs* to *desktop* and *disks*, respectively. Status dominates singularity: the writer ought to give the full formal name of the association the first time it is mentioned, but use the acronym the second time to minimize unnecessary repetition. On the other hand, the writer ought to give the full formal name of the journal both times it is mentioned because the journal is the topic of the article.

4. *Is the verbal style consistent across the lexical, grammatical, and mechanical levels of the discourse?*
Given the decisions registered in the style guide (see Figure 4.25), the verbal style of this discourse is consistent across all levels of the discourse.

Visual Propriety

1. *What are the visual style characteristics of discourse medium and participation, province, status, and modality?*
See Figure 4.26. Pertinent photographs often accompany the news. With this article, a dynamic and detailed picture of the operation of the equipment is appropriate, if available. It might, however, be difficult to obtain a genuinely informative or impressive picture.

2. *What are the visual style characteristics of individuality, dialect, time, and singularity?*
See Figure 4.26. The writer is opposed to using a photograph of the equipment, considering it unnecessarily boring and distracting because it is impossible to picture this subject either comprehensively or dynamically.

Author:
I think a drawing is the best visual for this text: something connected to writing that students will think intriguing.

The Writing Specialization
Texas A&M University

Because of the growing demand for highly skilled, professionally competent writers in business, industry, and government, the student with training in writing, speaking, ~~and~~ editing ~~and communication skills~~ has improved job opportunities. Often the individual who possesses such ~~skills~~ *abilities not only* gets a job sooner ~~and~~ *but also* advances faster ~~than~~ ~~someone without those skills~~ *Every professional--* The biologist writing an environmental impact report, the computer specialist designing a user's manual for new software, or the acccountant explaining an auditing procedure to a client-- ~~every professional~~ must be able to communicate ideas effectively and efficiently.

The Writing Specialization is a program designed to give students in business, scientific, technical, or humanistic disciplines (eighteen) hours of intensive training in a broad range of communication skills. Students who achieve a grade of B or better in all (eighteen) hours of coursework will receive a certificate signifying their successful completion of this training.

All students choosing this program will take (four) core courses:

English 210, Argumentation and Composition: the evaluation and composition of arguments through an intensive study of the logical processes of induction and deduction and the techniques of persuasion;

Figure 4.27. Editing a promotional publication for propriety.

English 301, Technical Writing: writing proposals,
memos, letters, and various types of business and technical reports for specialist and non-specialist audiences;

English 320, Technical Editing: *the* study and practice
of the rhetorical skills required of professional editors, from copyediting and proofreading to document
design and desktop publishing;

Speech Communication 404, Technical and Professional Speaking: composing and delivering oral presentations of technical material using various media.

In addition, the students will select (six) hours of
supporting courses usually connected with the student's
major. Students, in consultation with the Writing Specialization Coordinator in the Department of English, can
thereby create their own program of special emphasis.

To register for the The Writing Specialization or
to receive more information about it, contact Sam Dragga
(409-845-8304), 201D Blocker Building, Department of
English, Texas A&M University, College Station, TX 77843.

Figure 4.27. Editing a promotional publication for propriety (cont'd).

3. *Do the visual style characteristics of discourse medium and participation, province, status, and modality dominate the visual style characteristics of individuality, dialect, time, and singularity?*
Status and modality here accord with singularity: only a dynamic photograph of the subject is desirable, and none is available.

4. *Is the visual style consistent across the illustrations of the discourse?*
According to the decisions registered in the style guide (see again Figure 4.25), the visual style is consistent across the illustrations of the discourse.

	Lexical	Grammatical	Mechanical
Individuality	word repetition: e.g., *skills*	varied phrasing of listed items	
Dialect			
Time			
Singularity	repetition of possessive noun to avoid sexist pronouns and *his/her*	pairing of items: e.g., "effectively and efficiently"	spells numbers for formality
Discourse Medium and Participation	minimal redundancy	parallel phrasing of listed items, no complicated introductory lists, variety of sentences	
Province			numerals for credit hours and courses
Status	varied wording, plurals avoid sexist usage noun repetition, and *his/her*	parallel phrasing of listed items, variety of sentences	no complicated introductory lists
Modality	positive and concise wording		

Figure 4.28. Verbal style matrix for the promotional publication.

A	
B	
C	
D	
E	
F	
G	
H	
I	
J	
K	
L	
M	
N	
O	
P	
Q	
R	
S	plural *students*, if pronoun substitution is necessary
T	
U	
V	
W	
X,Y,Z	
1,2,3	18 hours, 4 courses, English 210
Informative/intriguing drawings	

Figure 4.29. Style guide for the promotional publication.

	Tables	Figures (nonpictorial-pictorial)
Individuality		
Dialect		
Time		
Singularity		likes the creativity of a drawing; sees it as similar to writing
Discourse medium and participation		
Province		interesting drawing; might be tough to focus attention on writing in a photo
Status		photo for impressiveness
Modality		interesting drawing or photo, if available and worthwhile

Figure 4.30. Visual style matrix for the promotional publication.

A Promotional Publication

This sample of a promotional publication is distributed by the Department of English, Texas A&M University (see Figure 4.27).

Verbal Propriety

1. *What are the verbal style characteristics of discourse medium and participation, province, status, and modality?*
See Figure 4.28. Because this is a persuasive written communication directed to students, it is essential that the message be direct, simple, and motivating.
2. *What are the verbal style characteristics of individuality, dialect, time, and singularity?*
See Figure 4.28. This writer strives for a degree of formality by frequently pairing grammatical structures and by spelling numbers.
3. *Do the verbal style characteristics of discourse medium and participation, province, status, and modality dominate the verbal style characteristics of individuality, dialect, time, and singularity?*
Province dominates singularity on the mechanical level: the conventions of the academic profession prescribe correction of the writer's spelling of numbers. On the grammatical level; discourse medium and participation as well as status recommend parallel phrasing of the course descriptions. Variety, however, is also important to keep readers attentive to the subject. Here a compromise of alternating parallel structures is possible, thereby making the four listed items obviously equivalent without the risk of a dulling repetition. This is also in accord with the author's frequent pairing of adjectives, nouns, verbs, phrases, and clauses. Variety is also important on the lexical level.
4. *Is the verbal style consistent across the lexical, grammatical, and mechanical levels of the discourse?*
Given the decisions registered in the style guide (see Figure 4.29), the verbal style of this discourse is consistent across all levels of the discourse.

Visual Propriety

1. *What are the visual style characteristics of discourse medium and participation, province, status, and modality?*
See Figure 4.30. Promotional publications often incorporate attractive photographs or drawings. Given the subject of this publication, it might be difficult to acquire a stirring photograph that symbolizes this professional writing program: that is, realistic photographs of a pencil or a word processor, with all their ordinary distracting details, are unlikely to stimulate

the reader's imagination, whereas vivid drawings of the identical items might be captivating.

2. *What are the visual style characteristics of individuality, dialect, time, and singularity?*

(See Figure 4.30.) The writer likes the creativity of drawings and considers this artistic activity a metaphor of the composing process. Moreover, the uniqueness and simplicity of a drawing give it memorability; a vivid drawing might thus serve as the logo of the Writing Specialization.

3. *Do the visual style characteristics of discourse medium and participation, province, status, and modality dominate the visual style characteristics of individuality, dialect, time, and singularity?*

Province and modality accord with singularity: drawings that symbolize the Writing Specialization prove especially fitting to this promotional publication.

4. *Is the visual style consistent across the illustrations of the discourse?*

According to the decisions registered in the style guide (see again Figure 4.29), the visual style is consistent across the illustrations of the discourse.

REFERENCES

1. E. P. J. Corbett, *Classical Rhetoric for the Modern Student*, 2nd edition, Oxford University Press, New York, 1971.
2. E. Lindemann, *A Rhetoric for Writing Teachers*, Oxford University Press, New York, 1982.
3. F. I. Hill, The Rhetoric of Aristotle, in *A Synoptic History of Classical Rhetoric*, J. J. Murphy (ed.), Hermagoras Press, Davis, California, pp. 90–150, 1983.
4. D. J. Ochs, Cicero's Rhetorical Theory, in *A Synoptic History of Classical Rhetoric*, J. J. Murphy (Ed.), Hermagoras Press, Davis, California, pp. 90–150, 1983.
5. P. A. Meador Jr., Quintilian and the *Institutio oratoria*, in *A Synoptic History of Classical Rhetoric*, J. J. Murphy (ed.), Hermagoras Press, Davis, California, pp. 151–176, 1983.
6. R. A. Lanham, *Revising Business Prose*, Scribner's, New York, 1981.
7. D. Crystal and D. Davy, *Investigating English Style*, Indiana University Press, Bloomington, 1969.
8. N. Sommers, Responding to Student Writing, *College Composition and Communication, 33*, pp. 148–156, 1982.

CHAPTER 5

Delivery

RHETORICAL THEORY OF DELIVERY

The final canon of rhetoric is delivery, traditionally associated with oral discourse only. Aristotle gives little attention to this subject, with a brief and apologetic discussion of voice and the importance of the speaker's volume and pitch. Cicero, however, sees delivery as "precepts to guide the physical presentation of the text" [1, p. 93] and emphasizes this as critical to the eloquence of the discourse. According to Cicero, delivery is elocution, comprising gesticulation and facial expression as well as the register and intensity of the speaker's voice. Effective delivery is flexible, adjusted to the subject and style of the discourse, and thus assures that the speaker is perceived as sincere. Quintilian also emphasizes delivery as elocution, and it is professional speakers who develop and discuss the skills of elocution during the Middle Ages and the Renaissance.

Because delivery is given this emphasis, discussions of written discourse have typically ignored this canon of rhetoric. Unlike the numerous conventions for the oral presentation of texts prescribed by elocutionists, as a consequence, accurate and legible printing exist as virtually the only standards for the effective delivery of the written discourse produced by professional scribes. So that the text might be aesthetically inspiring as well as functional, each scribe would liberally embellish it with distinctive artistic designs and decorative innovations.

With the invention of the printing press comes little or no immediate change in the design of written discourse: the earliest typescripts imitate the manuscripts of the scribes. Beginning with the rise of literacy and the technological advances of the Industrial Revolution, however, there is a revival of delivery and a new perspective on the written text and its physical presentation, especially with news and promotional publications. As the technology associated with written communication has evolved, attention to the canon of delivery has flourished.

Rhetorical choices associated with delivery were previously restricted to businesses which could manage the high costs of professional designing and publishing. With computer technology, the costs have decreased and more and more individuals have access to important delivery choices. For example, fifty years ago, the individual who wished to create a text was limited to a typewriter and its limited repertoire of typographic characters: that is, either pica or elite type, upper and lower case letters, and underlining. The invention of the electric typewriter with a changeable typing element brought additional access (though fairly expensive and inconvenient) to a number of different typefaces. The word processor with dot-matrix or letter-quality printer allowed boldfacing. And current desktop publishing systems (i.e., a microcomputer and laser printer) permit the wide variety of typefaces, typesizes, and typestyles and the integration of illustrations previously available only through professional printing services.

More and more writers and editors, as a consequence, find themselves facing a wide array of delivery choices. A major source of guidelines on the canon of delivery has been the handbook tradition [2, p. 64]: typically, this is a series of mechanical prescriptions on the width of margins, the spacing between lines, the size and weight of paper, the design of tables and figures, etc. In addition, professional experience through trial and error yields a sense of rhetorical effectiveness, of the artistry of rhetoric. And more and more rhetoricians, reading specialists, psychologists, philosophers, semiologists, and artists have been researching the human perception of written discourse. A major theorist on this subject is Jacques Bertin, who discusses visual characteristics which can guide editors and writers in analyzing and designing the physical presentation of a text.

Visual Variables

According to Bertin, the human eye is sensitive to six visual or retinal variables; *size, value* (i.e., lightness/darkness), *texture* (i.e., various densities and patterns of dots and lines), *color, orientation* (i.e., horizontal, vertical, diagonal, etc.), and *shape* (i.e., rectangular, circular, oval, triangular, etc.). The retinal variables also have semantic properties. A retinal variable is *associated* if it allows the grouping of similar signs [3, p. 65]. In Figure 5.1, for example, the reader visually categorizes the signs according to their shape, as circles, ovals, squares, or rectangles. The retinal variable of shape is therefore associated. Size, however, is disassociated. In Figure 5.2, for example, the reader might still wish to categorize the signs according to their shape only; however, the big and small circles proscribe that categorization. This is because dissociated variables dominate associated variables: that is, the reader notices big and small circles instead of just circles. Though it is impossible to group the signs according to their size only, the size differences leave it equally impossible to perceive the signs according to their shape only.

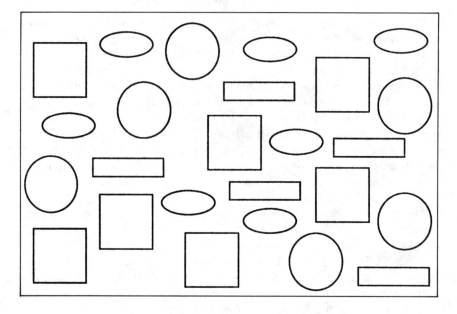

Figure 5.1. Associated variables.

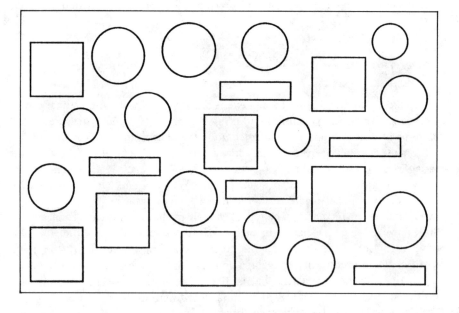

Figure 5.2. Dissociated variables.

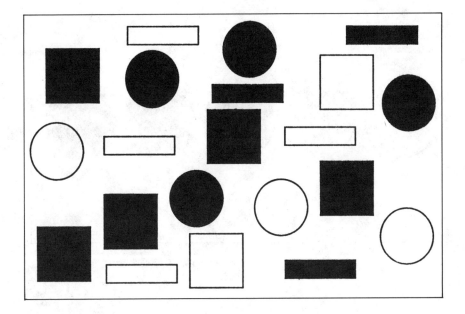

Figure 5.3. Selective variables.

Figure 5.4. Non-selective variables.

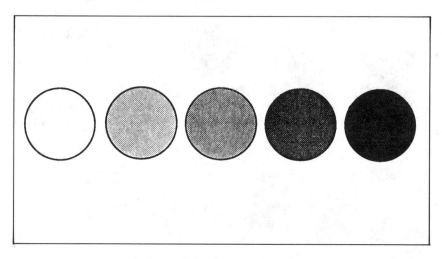

Figure 5.5. Ordered variables.

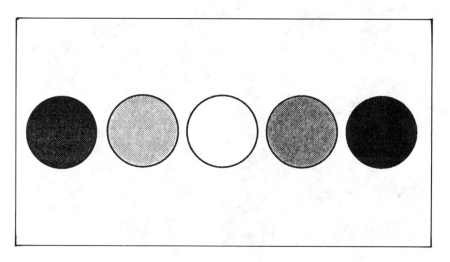

Figure 5.6. Disordered variables.

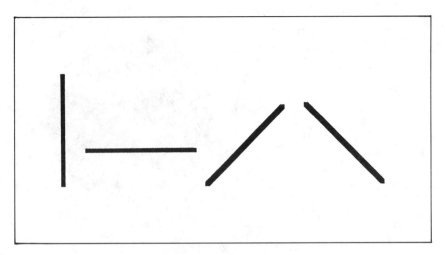

Figure 5.7. Unordered variables.

If a retinal variable allows the reader to isolate all occurrences of a sign and ignore different signs, it is *selective* [3, p. 67]. Figure 5.3, for example, shows black and white squares, circles, and rectangles. The reader can ignore all the black objects and focus only on all the white objects, or vice versa. Value is selective. In Figure 5.4, however, the reader finds it impossible to ignore all the circles and rectangles and focus only on all the squares. The retinal variable of shape is without selectivity.

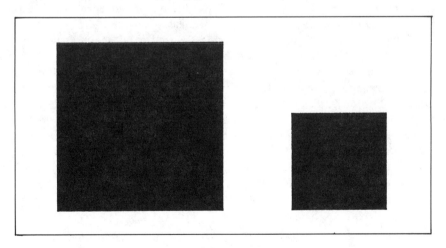

Figure 5.8. Proportional variables.

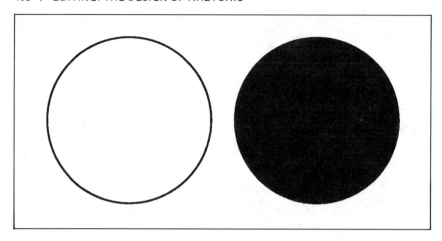

Figure 5.9. Non-proportional variables.

A variable is *ordered* if it allows the reader to perceive the hierarchy of its occurrences [3, p. 67]. For example, the different textures of the circles in Figure 5.5, indicate that the hierarchy of importance is either left to right or right to left. The relationship among the circles is clear. If shown the circles of Figure 5.6, the reader immediately ascribes to them the ranking of Figure 5.5. The series of lines in Figure 5.7 have no similar relationship: there is no recognition of the vertical line as more or less important than the horizontal line or the horizontal line as more or less important than the diagonal. Orientation is unordered.

A retinal variable is *proportional* if quantitative or numerical meaning is attributed to it [3, p. 69]. The only proportional variable is size. For example, given the big and small squares of Figure 5.8 and a big number and small number, readers always associate the big number with the big square and the small number with the small square. No similar association occurs with different shapes, orientations, color, textures, or values. For example, given the different circles of Figure 5.9, the readers might ascribe a big or small number to the black circle and a big or small number to the white circle.

Figure 5.10 shows a matrix of the retinal variables and their corresponding semantic properties [3, p. 96]. Each variable has a unique mix of properties: this allows each variable to communicate the specific information it does and to serve a specific function in the physical presentation of discourse.

Shape

This variable communicates the single meaning of association: that is, shape allows the grouping of different objects, the symbolizing of different categories.

	Associated	Selective	Ordered	Proportional
Size		X	X	X
Value		X	X	
Texture	X	X	X	
Color	X	X		
Orientation	X	X		
Shape	X			

Figure 5.10.   Matrix of retinal variables.

This variable might occur, for example, on a city map, with squares signalling the location of schools and triangles indicating museums. Or illustrations might be given different shapes to reinforce categories: for example, oval photographs of tourist attractions versus circular photographs of shops and restaurants.

Orientation

This variable is selective as well as associated: that is, it allows grouping of objects *and* focusing on a single group. On a city map, this variable might occur as a cross (+) to symbolize every hospital and crossed diagonals (X) to designate every post office. A tourist examining the map would immediately perceive the different categories: in addition, by ignoring all the crosses, he or she could view the location of all post offices within the city.

Color

Similar to orientation, this variable is also selective and associated. In a maintenance and repair manual, for example, all repair information might be given in red type and all maintenance information in black type. Color thus serves to communicate the different categories of information within the manual and allows either random or sequential access to that information: that is, the user reading the manual might examine the maintenance and repair information as it occurs, or might examine all the maintenance information and then all the repair information or vice versa, or might examine only the maintenance

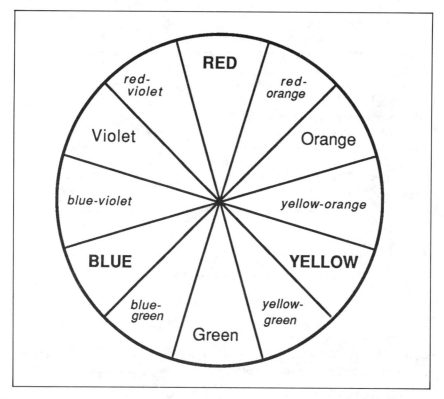

Figure 5.11. Color wheel.

information or only the repair information. In a discourse requiring sequential access only, color might thus be a serious distraction. For example, if the instructions of a user's manual were given in black type with the warnings or cautions corresponding to each instruction given in red type, the design of the discourse would allow the user to perceive the different categories of information and to ignore all the warnings. Coupling color and size (i.e., red type larger than the black type), however, would emphasize the importance of the cautionary information. That is, as a selective variable, color gives readers random access to information: if random access is undesirable, color might be omitted. If color is still important to the design of the discourse because of its associative characteristics, color must be linked to the ordered and proportional variable of size.

The variable of color is also complicated by the multiplicity of colors which occur and their combination with the ordered variable of value: that is, colors differ in their degree of lightness and darkness [3, p. 85]. The color wheel (see Figure 5.11) shows the primary colors of red, yellow and blue. Mixing the primary colors yields the secondary colors of orange, green, and violet; mixing the primary and secondary colors yields the tertiary or intermediate colors of red-orange, yellow-orange, yellow-green, blue-green, blue-violet and red-violet. At full saturation or purity, yellow is the lightest of colors (i.e., a minimum of blackness); the secondary colors adjacent to yellow are darker, and the tertiary colors adjacent to them even darker [4, pp. 17-18]. The darkest colors (i.e., a minimum of whiteness) are red and blue and the secondary and tertiary colors between them [4, pp. 17-18]. Adding white or black to a color is also possible: for example, pink is a mix of white and red, and maroon a mix of black and red. Though color is only associated and selective, this link between color and the ordered variable of value has important design implications. In a pie chart using color, for example, with three pieces to the pie—red, yellow, and blue—the equally dark colors of red and blue might be perceived, especially during a quick scanning, as a single piece of pie versus the light (yellow) piece. It might thus be essential to the clarity of the illustration that the bigger each piece is, the lighter its color is (or the smaller each piece, the lighter its color).

Simultaneously, blue and the secondary and tertiary colors adjacent to it, have the shortest wavelengths of light, whereas red and yellow and the secondary and tertiary colors between them have the longest wavelengths [5, pp. 55-57]. This is why blues and greens, typically called "cool" colors, seem to recede and look small or distant, while the "hot" colors such as red and orange seem to advance and look big or close [5, p. 219].

The relationship between different colors is also a critical design consideration. Complementary colors occur as opposites on the color wheel (see Figure 5.11): for example, red and green, blue and orange, yellow and violet. A color elicits its complement in all colors to which it is adjacent: for example, red adjoining yellow-green causes the yellow-green to look greener, and blue adjoining yellow gives the yellow a distinct orange tinge.

Texture

This is the only associated variable which is also ordered. This allows the simultaneous ranking and categorizing of subjects. As a selective variable, texture gives additional focused access to information. In an alphabetical listing of college professors, for example, bullets of progressively denser texture might indicate the names of assistant professors, associate professors, and full professors. The different bullets thus identify the different categories of professors and indicate their hierarchy; by focusing on bullets of a single texture, the reader sees only the professors of a specific rank. A listing thus designed gives the reader multiple access: alphabetical, categorical, and hierarchical. In addition, texture is often linked to value: that is, changes in texture yield variations in lightness or darkness, or vice versa.

Value

Linked to the associated variables of color and texture and the proportional variable of size, this ordered and selective variable is especially appropriate to the hierarchical organization of information. In written discourse, for example, bold headings signal their superiority and solicit immediate attention, establishing their clear dominance over the greyness of the paragraphs and the white spaces of the page. It is also possible to ignore the grey paragraphs, focus only on the bold headings, and thus glance through the discourse: this is typical of the initial reading given newspapers and magazines. A bold letter, however, is also bigger and thicker: the bigger size also shows its higher ranking, and its thicker textures allows the association of all bold letters versus all plain letters. And a difference of lightness or darkness, as mentioned earlier, does characterize different colors (e.g., red and blue versus yellow) and distinguish between colors (e.g., red versus pink): as a consequence, letters of different value (e.g., bold versus plain) can be associated according to their different colors (e.g., black versus grey).

Size

This is the only variable that is proportional and thus uniquely appropriate to the communication of numerical or statistical information. In a bar graph, for example, it is only the size of each bar that signals its quantitative meaning. Simultaneously, size is selective and ordered: it is therefore possible to observe or ignore things according to their size, assign a priority to things according to their size, and link quantitative differences to qualitative differences (e.g., the bigger the picture or heading, the more important it is).

The matrix of six retinal variables and their corresponding semantic properties gives writers and editors a way of perceiving the artistry with which written discourse is delivered, a way of judging the efficacy of the classic ad hoc guidelines on design. It is our purpose in this chapter thus to balance the wisdom and experience of professional editors with rhetorical theory and research on delivery. In doing so, we examine four major subjects: 1) typography; 2) illustrations; 3) page design; and 4) production processes.

Typography

Because typography is a dominant characteristic of the majority of written discourse, the rhetorical effect of type is a vital consideration for editors. It is therefore critical that the editor's typographical choices harmonize with the communicative aim and audience of the discourse. And the editor has a wide variety of designs, sizes, and styles of type among which to choose.

Designs

Type is categorized as either *serif* or *sans serif*. Serif type has additional horizontal lines at the top or bottom of the major vertical strokes of letters, whereas sans serif type omits these lines:

This is an example of serif type.

This is an example of sans serif type.

There are two major reasons for choosing serif or sans serif typeface: aesthetic appeal and readability. Serif type seems artistic, designed with grace and flourish; sans serif types looks clean, objective, direct. In addition, it is widely thought that serif letters improve readability: the horizontal serifs seem to link the letters and guide the eye across the page [6, pp. 8-9; 7, pp. 128-131]. In the verbally oriented discourse of the humanities, this is especially important. For example in the field of philosophy, the typical text is exclusively verbal: the reader is expected to read from start to finish without stopping, and paragraphing is the only indicator of the divisions within the discourse. Technical and business professionals, however, often prefer sans serif type: typically their texts are visually oriented, giving the reader random access to the information by displaying it within localized blocks, using headings liberally. Horizontal guiding of the eye is less critical because the toil of reading is periodically interrupted with illustrations, and eye fatigue is thus less likely to occur.

The design of serifs is also distinctive: basically, however, serifs might be categorized as either curved or straight and with a pointed or circular ending:

EIbdjpy   EIbdjpy   EIbdjpy   EIbdjpy

In addition to the presence or absence of serifs, the design of type differs according to the following characteristics (see Figure 5.12).

The *x-height* is the vertical measure of the body of all lower case letters, as exemplified by the lower case *x*. There is considerable variation in the x-height of different typefaces:

lxH lxH lxH lxH lxH lxH

A *counter* is the enclosed space in the design of various letters. Counters can be horizontally or vertically narrow or wide:

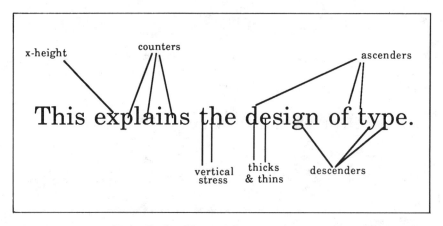

Figure 5.12.   Characteristics of type design.

Bdeg Bdeg Bdeg Bdeg Bdeg Bdeg

An *ascender* is the vertical line that extends above the x-height of a lowercase letter:

bhkf bhkf bhkf bhkf bhkf bhkf

Typically the height of ascenders is equal to the height of upper case letters. In typefaces with serifs, the intersection of the ascender and the serif is either curved or angled.

A *descender* is the vertical line that extends below the body (x-height) of a lowercase letter:

jpyg jpyg jpyg jpyg jpyg jpyg

In typefaces with serifs, the intersection of the descender and the serif is either curved or angled.

Thicks and thins are the heavy and light lines which compose a letter. The width of thicks and thins differs considerably across typefaces, from no difference to quite wide thicks and quite narrow thins:

AWzk AWzk AWzk AWzk AWzk AWzk

Vertical stress is the emphasis given to thick vertical lines versus thin horizontal lines in the design of a letter. A typeface with heavy vertical stress has its thicker lines running vertically and its thinner lines running horizontally, whereas a typeface with light vertical stress shows little difference in the width of horizontal and vertical lines:

FLhm FLhm FLhm FLhm FLhm FLhm

Together, the six design characteristics give each typeface a distinctive texture (see Figure 5.13). Because the retinal variable of texture is associated, using the same typeface throughout a document signals to the reader that the information in the text is unified, that the different blocks of information have a common denominator. Texture, however, is also a selective and ordered variable. Using different typefaces, as a consequence, often yields a disjointed and incoherent document. The reader focuses on isolated blocks of information and thus perceives the blocks as disparate. Simultaneously, he or she strives to justify or ascribe a logical ordering to the different blocks of information: reading is strained or stopped because focus shifts to interpreting the design of the discourse as opposed to the discourse itself.

Sizes

Each typeface comes in a wide range of sizes. Type size or height is measured in points, with 12 points to a pica, and 6 picas to the inch (or 72 points to the inch). A type size of 10 or 12 points is common. This size refers to the height of the type body: that is, the traditional piece of lead alloy on which the typeface itself sits (see Figure 5.14). The height of the typeface is never the same as the height of the type body: therefore, typefaces of equal points often differ in size (see Figure 5.15). Because size is a proportional and ordered variable, it signals the relative importance of various blocks of discourse: for example, a 24-point heading is obviously superior to a 12-point heading. And the selectivity of size allows the isolation of equally important blocks of discourse.

Styles

All the upper and lower case letters and symbols of a given design and size compose a font of type (see Figure 5.16). Every font offers a variety of different styles: for example, plain, bold, italic, outline, shadow (see Figure 5.17). Each type style has a distinctive texture or value, and italics has the unique trait of its special orientation. The editor's choice of type style, as a consequence, is critical to effective reading. For example, the typical reader associates blocks of discourse according to their orientations and textures: therefore, associated

Because the retinal variable of texture is associated, using the same typeface throughout a document signals to the reader that the information in the text is unified, that the different blocks of information have a common denominator. Texture, however, is also a selective and ordered variable. Using different typefaces, as a consequence, often yields a disjointed and incoherent document. The reader focuses on isolated blocks of information and thus perceives the blocks as disparate.

Because the retinal variable of texture is associated, using the same typeface throughout a document signals to the reader that the information in the text is unified, that the different blocks of information have a common denominator. Texture, however, is also a selective and ordered variable. Using different typefaces, as a consequence, often yields a disjointed and incoherent document. The reader focuses on isolated blocks of information and thus perceives the blocks as disparate.

Because the retinal variable of texture is associated, using the same type-face throughout a document signals to the reader that the information in the text is unified, that the different blocks of information have a common denominator. Texture, however, is also a selective and ordered variable. Using different typefaces, as a consequence, often yields a disjointed and incoherent document. The reader focuses on isolated blocks of information and thus perceives the blocks as disparate.

Figure 5.13. The textures of different typefaces.

blocks of information ought to display similar styles of type, such as italic or plain. Similarly, readers perceive variations of value as signalling the hierarchy of disclosure blocks: therefore, changes of plain to bold ought to correspond clearly to the order of importance or urgency. Arbitrary or sporadic changes of type style only prove distracting and disorienting.

In addition each type style can occur as either a positive (i.e., black on white) or negative (i.e., white on black) image (see Figure 5.18). Reading a positive image is easier because black letters absorb 97% or more of the surrounding

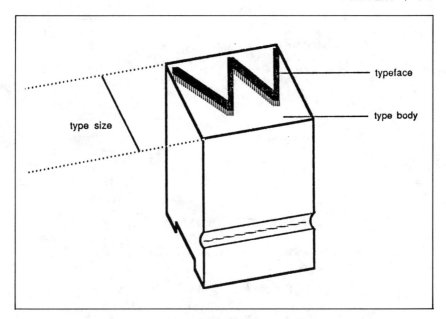

Figure 5.14. A traditional piece of type.

9 point	X	X	X	X	X	X
10 point	X	X	X	X	X	X
12 point	X	X	X	X	X	X
14 point	X	X	X	X	X	X
18 point	X	X	X	X	X	X
24 point	X	X	X	X	X	X

Figure 5.15. Sizes of different typefaces.

ABCDEFGHIJKLMNOPQRSTUVWXYZ
abcdefghijklmnopqrstuvwxyz
1234567890~`!@#$%^&*()-_=+[]{}:;"<,>.?/|\
¡™£¢∞§¶•ªº–≠œ∑´®†¥¨^øπ"'åß∂ƒ©˙∆˚¬ …æΩ≈ç√∫~µ≤≥÷
«»/□◊fi‡°·,—±Œ„‰ÂÊÁËÈØ∏""ÅÍÎÏÌÓÔÒÚÆÛÙÇ◊ı^¯˘¿

Figure 5.16.   A font of type.

This is a sans serif typeface in plain style.

This is a sans serif typeface in bold style.

This is a sans serif typeface in italic style.

This is a sans serif typeface in bold italic style.

This is a sans serif typeface in outline style.

This is a sans serif typeface in bold outline style.

This is a sans serif typeface in italic outline style.

This is a sans serif typeface in bold italic outline style.

This is a sans serif typeface in shadow style.

This is a sans serif typeface in bold shadow style.

This is a sans serif typeface in italic shadow style.

This is a sans serif typeface in bold italic shadow style.

Figure 5.17.   Styles of type.

Each type style can occur as either a positive (i.e., black on white) image or as a negative (i.e., white on black) image. Reading is easier, however, if the image is positive. Editors ordinarily limit negative images to brief passages requiring special emphasis, using a sans serif typeface and a large size of type.

Each type style can occur as either a positive (i.e., black on white) image or as a negative (i.e., white on black) image. Reading is easier, however, if the image is positive. Editors ordinarily limit negative images to brief passages requiring special emphasis, using a sans serif typeface and a large size of type.

Figure 5.18. Positive and negative images.

light and thus always look equally black and crisp. In negative or reverse images, however, the white letters reflect 80% or more of the light illuminating them: as a consequence, the image on which the eye tries to focus seems itself to emit light [4, p. 16]. In addition, the brightness of the negative image varies considerably with the available lighting, and this variation in brightness obscures the definition of the letters: that is, the less bright the negative image, the less distinct it is [4, p. 16]. Because readers encounter more difficulty focusing on the letters of a negative image and because reading is therefore slowed, editors restrict the use of negative images, choosing sans serif typefaces and large typesizes for brief passages that require special emphasis [8, pp. 131–137].

Type styles, as well as positive and negative images, can also occur in a variety of colors. Unlike the achromatic colors of black and white, which reflect and absorb all wavelengths of light equally, the chromatic colors reflect and absorb only their characteristic wavelengths of light [4, p. 16]. This reduces the contrast between light reflected and light absorbed, or between light and dark. To compensate for this reduction in contrast, editors ordinarily use color only for special emphasis, often choosing a large typesize and a sans serif typeface.

In addition, shifts from positive to negative images yield changes in the value and texture of the discourse. This allows readers to group, select, and order blocks of discourse according to their image: for example, brief warnings or headings might occur as negative images. In texts using color, similarly, readers can categorize and choose blocks of discourse according to this retinal variable.

This paragraph is easy to read because it has upper and lower case letters. The ascenders and descenders on lower case letters aid the reader's recognition and identification of individual letters.

THIS PARAGRAPH IS DIFFICULT TO READ BECAUSE IT IS ALL UPPERCASE LETTERS. BECAUSE OF THE UNIFORM SIZE, IDENTIFICATION OF INDIVIDUAL LETTERS IS SLOWED AND READING IS STRAINED.

Figure 5.19. Upper and lower case letters.

Variations of size as well as value and texture can occur within a type style through the editor's choice of upper or lower case letters (see Figure 5.19). The size of the upper case letters signals their priority over lower case letters. Ironically, however, the retinal variables of upper case letters—size, value, texture, and shape—appear uniform, and the eye therefore associates the individual letters instead of distinguishing between them. This slows reading, and therefore the use of upper case letters is ordinarily restricted to brief passages and headings [8, pp. 57-61]. In lower case letters, however, the characteristic ascenders and descenders aid the reader's recognition and identification of individual letters.

Spacing

Typefaces of equal vertical size often differ in the horizontal spacing between letters and words (see Figure 5.20). This spacing changes the texture and value of a block of discourse: that is, readers associate, select, and order passages according to visual density. If horizontal spacing is too tight, the eye has difficulty identifying individual words, but sees instead a continuous string of letters. If, however, horizontal spacing is too loose, the eye sees isolated letters and has difficulty grouping the letters in order to perceive words; grouping words in order to perceive phrases is also impaired because the horizontal progression of the eye across the page is interrupted by vertical rivers of white space. It is also possible to adjust horizontal spacing, a process called *kerning*. Each typeface gives each of its letters a characteristic width and spacing between adjoining letters: as a consequence, various pairs of letters might require kerning (see Figure 5.21).

Variations in typesize, typestyle, letterspacing, or wordspacing yield a corresponding variation in the number of letters which occupy a given line length. This

If horizontal spacing is too tight, the eye has difficulty identifying individual words, but sees instead a continuous string of letters. If, however, horizontal spacing is too loose, the eye sees isolated letters and has difficulty grouping the letters in order to perceive words; grouping words in order to perceive phrases is also impaired because the horizontal progression of the eye across the page is interrupted by vertical rivers of white space.

If horizontal spacing is too tight, the eye has difficulty identifying individual words, but sees instead a continuous string of letters. If, however, horizontal spacing is too loose, the eye sees isolated letters and has difficulty grouping the letters in order to perceive words; grouping words in order to perceive phrases is also impaired because the horizontal progression of the eye across the page is interrupted by vertical rivers of white space.

Figure 5.20.   Horizontal spacing.

count of the letters is ordinarily given per linear inch or per pica and is often called the pitch or character count: for example, 12-point Helvetica plain type with tight spacing has a character count of 16, whereas 12-point Helvetica bold type with tight spacing has a count of 12, as does 12-point Helvetica plain type with loose spacing.

A character count is a major indicator of the vertical and horizontal space a given block of discourse requires. For example, a 250-word text has approxi-

	before	after
inserting space	Wh gy ft	Wh gy ft
deleting space	Yo We P.	Yo We P.

Figure 5.21.   Kerning.

This paragraph is displayed in 10-point **sans serif** type with **one point** of leading. Leading is especially important to the readability of sans serif typefaces, typefaces with a large x-height or heavy vertical stress, and longer line lengths.

This paragraph is displayed in 10-point **sans serif** type with **two points** of leading. Leading is especially important to the readability of sans serif typefaces, typefaces with a large x-height or heavy vertical stress, and longer line lengths.

This paragraph is displayed in a 10-point serif typeface with a large **x-height and a heavy vertical stress**. It uses **one point** of leading. Leading is especially important to the readability of sans serif typefaces, typefaces with a large x-height or heavy vertical stress, and longer line lengths.

This paragraph is displayed in a 10-point serif typeface with a large **x-height and a heavy vertical stress**. It uses **two points** of leading. Leading is especially important to the readability of sans serif typefaces, typefaces with a large x-height or heavy vertical stress, and longer line lengths.

Figure 5.22. Paired examples of one- and two-point leading.

mately 1500 characters (i.e., 5 characters per word plus a 1-character space); a type with a character count of 12 requires 125 linear inches or 750 picas. If the line length is 5 inches or 30 picas, the text requires 25 lines. (Similarly, given a specific length or number of lines, it is also possible to determine the necessary character count.)

The ideal line length differs according to the communicative aim and audience of the discourse as well as the size, style, and design of the type. News publications, for example, typically have three to six narrow columns and line lengths of approximately 30 characters, whereas a longer line of roughly 70 characters is suitable for the professional readership of technical publications. In addition, factors which aid readability (e.g., serifs, positive image, upper/lower case) justify a longer line, whereas characteristics which diminish readability (e.g., sans serifs, small size, negative image, all caps) deserve a shorter line.

The space between consecutive lines is called leading. This and type size determine the vertical space which lines of type occupy. This measure is usually given as type size over type size with leading. For example, 10/12 indicates 10-point type occupying a 12-point vertical space (i.e., 10 points of type with 2 points of leading). Leading is especially important to the readability of sans serif

This paragraph is **left aligned**, ragged right. It is widely thought that this allows the easiest reading because the beginning of each line has a similar location, the wordspacing is equal across the page, and the unequal line length both keeps readers attentive and helps them to distinguish between consecutive lines of type and thereby avoid double readings.

This paragraph is **justified**. While justified type yields a symmetrical block of discourse and thus is initially pleasing to the eye, its unequal wordspacing and the resulting vertical rivers of white space often diminish its readability. In addition, with each line of equal length, the visual diversity of consecutive lines is forfeited and double reading, as a consequence, is likelier.

This paragraph is **right aligned**, ragged left. Type aligned on the right margin with the left side ragged is usually limited to special or brief passages and headings, in spite of its equal wordspacing and unequal line length. In languages reading left to right, right alignment is perceived as difficult because the location of the beginning of each line is different.

This paragraph is **centered** (i.e., ragged left and right). It has a limited currency and is usually associated with formality (e.g., wedding invitations). In spite of its equal wordspacing and unequal line length, reading is difficult because the location of the beginning of each line is different.

Figure 5.23. Examples of different type alignments.

typefaces, typefaces with a large x-height or heavy vertical stress, and longer line lengths [8, p. 129] (see Figure 5.22). The common type sizes of 10 and 12 points average one or two points of leading, with smaller and larger sizes usually requiring at least two points.

Also important to the reader's perception of written discourse is its alignment on the page (see Figure 5.23). In languages reading left to right, type is ordinarily aligned on the left margin with the right side remaining ragged. It is widely thought that this allows the easiest reading because the beginning of each line has a similar location, the wordspacing is equal across the page, and the unequal line length both keeps readers attentive and helps them to distinguish between consecutive lines of type and thereby avoid double readings.

Also widely occurring is justified type: that is, type aligned on the left and right margins. While justified type yields a symmetrical block of discourse and thus is initially pleasing to the eye, its unequal wordspacing and the resulting vertical rivers of white space often diminish its readability. This is especially obvious with narrow columns of type. In addition, with each line of equal length, the visual diversity of consecutive lines is forfeited and double reading, as a consequence, is likelier.

Type aligned on the right margin with the left side ragged is usually limited to special or brief passages and headings, in spite of its equal wordspacing and unequal line length. In languages reading left to right, right alignment is perceived as difficult because the location of the beginning of each line is different. Of equal reading difficulty is centered type (i.e., ragged left and right). It also has a limited currency and is usually associated with formality (e.g., wedding invitations).

Character counts, line lengths, leading, and alignment together determine the vertical and horizontal space necessary to display a block of discourse and offer the editor a variety of sizes, values, textures, and shapes for the design of that discourse. Each of the editor's decisions on type spacing, as a consequence, has significance. For example, the typical reader associates blocks of discourse according to their shapes and textures: therefore associated blocks of information ought to display similar alignments or leading. Similarly, news publications often run stories in 15-pica columns and editorials in 30-pica columns, and readers identify the different line lengths with the shift of communicative aim. If the editor's change of type spacing is arbitrary or erratic, effective reading is interrupted or strained.

Illustrations

In the delivery of verbal information, the editor chooses a typographical design which satisfies the communicative aim and audience of the discourse. The delivery of visual information requires the editor to design equally satisfactory illustrations. In doing so, the editor considers the import of the retinal variables, exploiting their semantic properties and insuring that the variables reinforce each other and thus instruct and persuade the reader (instead of contradict each other and thereby confuse the reader).

Tables

As a verbally oriented illustration, a table exploits the same retinal variables that verbal discourse does—the retinal variables characteristic of typography, especially size, value, and texture. The aesthetic guidelines and readability considerations that determine the typography of verbal discourse, as a consequence, also apply to the design, style, size, and spacing of type in tables.

Ordinarily, the typeface of a table is the same as that of the text, thereby associating all information within the discourse. If, however, the editor wishes to emphasize a table or establish it as a self-contained block of discourse, he or she might exploit the variable of selectivity and change from a serif to a sans serif typeface (or vice versa). Variations of style and size guide the eye through the table itself: table headings, for example, often occur in a larger type size or bold type style to signify their dominance. And the alignment of information, as well as the spacing of columns and rows, proves essential to effective reading. For example, a column of numerals is always aligned on the decimal point, whereas a column of words is typically aligned on the left with a ragged right.

In addition to decisions on the typographical design of a table, the editor has illustrative choices. Boxing a table, for example, signals its formality and selectivity. Superimposing a table on a pertinent photograph or drawing reinforces the subject; superimposing a table on a corresponding chart or graph emphasizes especially important information.

Figures

Every illustration that is not a table, displaying information in columns and rows, is considered a figure. This definition indicates that the range of figures is wide—from the non-pictorial (e.g., graphs and charts) to the pictorial (e.g., drawings and photographs). Hybrid figures also occur (e.g., a graph superimposed on a pertinent photograph). Unlike verbally-oriented tables, figures are visually-oriented illustrations capitalizing on diverse combinations of the retinal variables. The human eye still moves left to right and top to bottom: however, the editor, by manipulating the variables, tries to design figures that encourage viewing as opposed to reading, that allow immediate understanding instead of slow deciphering.

Line Graphs

The design of graphs requires three kinds of lines: (1) the horizontal axis and vertical axis; (2) the grid lines; (3) the data lines. The horizontal axis usually signifies time (e.g., seconds, minutes, hours, days, months, years) and the vertical axis shows quantitative change over time (e.g., profits, sales, population). Clearly labeled tick marks intersect the axes and indicate regular intervals of time and standard quantitative measures (e.g., percentages, grams, meters); hash marks (i.e., paired diagonal slashes along either axis) signal an interruption in the scale, like ellipses in prose. The data lines begin on the vertical axis and cross the grid lines: distance from the vertical axis indicates duration; distance from the horizontal axis indicates quantity.

In a multiple line graph, the data lines are typically differentiated from each other and from the grid lines by color, value, size, or texture in order to help readers to distinguish between data lines and grid lines. This is especially important if there is little or no difference in the orientation of the grid and data lines

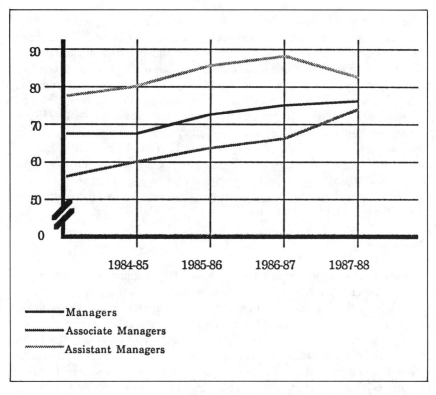

Figure 5.24. Multiple line graph with value and texture reinforcing hierarchy.

(i.e., if the data lines move parallel to the horizontal or vertical axis). Grid lines allow readers to pinpoint particular quantities at particular points in time. The absence of grid lines increases the white space and, as a consequence, emphasizes the data lines and their overall direction.

In Figure 5.24, the number of managers, associate managers, and assistant managers within a company is traced over a four-year period. As the key indicates, each data line represents a different level of management and thus varies in value and texture. In this multiple line graph, the ordered variables of texture and value reinforce the managerial hierarchy: that is, the denser the dot pattern (texture) and the darker the line (value), the higher the position in the company. The design of these lines thus enables readers to trace, compare, and interpret trends among these managerial groups over time. An editor could also accomplish this same effect by using colors with varying amounts of black or white to reinforce associated, selective, and ordered variables.

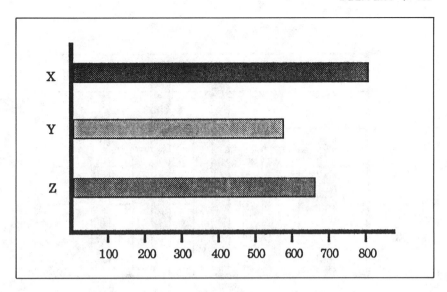

Figure 5.25. Bar chart with value and texture reinforcing size.

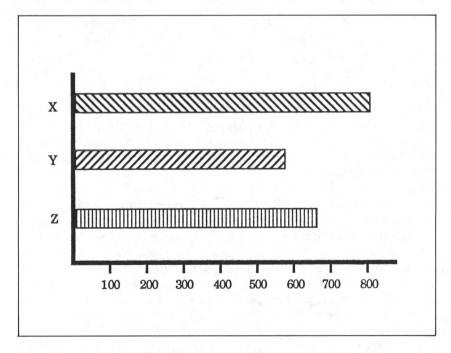

Figure 5.26. Bar chart with distracting textures.

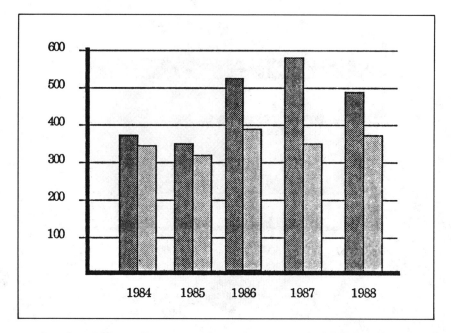

Figure 5.27. Column chart with consistent textures.

Bar Charts

Like the line graphs, bar charts enable readers to compare numerical quantities. Instead of representing changes over time through different data lines, however, quantities are illustrated through rectangular bars originating on the vertical axis and running parallel to the horizontal axis. Grid lines or tick marks intersect the horizontal axis only: distance from the vertical axis indicates quantity.

Ideally, the ordered variables of value and texture reinforce the ordered and proportional variable of size. That is, the longer the bar, the darker (or lighter) and finer (or coarser) it is (see Figure 5.25). To avoid misleading readers, however, the pattern used to indicate texture (e.g., dots, diagonals, concentric circles) is the same for all bars. This is because differing patterns often cause distracting optical illusions. For example, if a given bar has a pattern of diagonals with a left orientation and a neighboring bar has a pattern of diagonals with a right orientation, the bars themselves no longer appear parallel to the horizontal axis, but seem to adopt a diagonal orientation (see Figure 5.26). It is therefore more difficult for the reader to associate the bars, to perceive them as measuring comparable quantities. Likewise, if the bars are of equal width, the significance

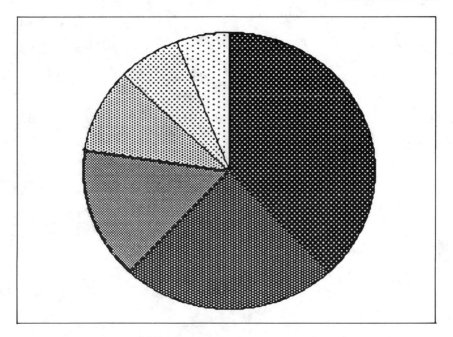

Figure 5.28.   Pie chart with value reinforcing size.

of their length is emphasized; the similarity of shape helps the reader to associate the bars, comparing and contrasting their lengths.

Column Charts

Column charts combine several of the characteristics of line graphs and bar charts. Instead of representing changes over time through different data lines, specific quantities are illustrated through rectangular columns originating on the horizontal axis and running parallel to the vertical axis. Grid lines or tick marks intersect the vertical axis only, and distance from the horizontal axis (i.e., the height of the column) indicates quantity.

The editor exploits the way a reader's eye moves across a figure by arranging columns chronologically from left to right and capitalizes on the associative variables of shape and texture by maintaining the same width and pattern (e.g., dots, diagonals, concentric circles) for all columns. Figure 5.27, for example, depicts the quantity of given commodities at several consecutive points in time.

Pie Charts

A pie chart is a circle which is divided into wedges to illustrate the various fractions of a whole. Wedges are arranged clockwise according to size, with the

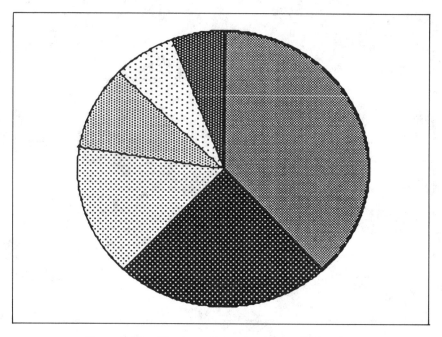

Figure 5.29.   Pie chart with value contradicting size.

biggest wedge traditionally beginning at twelve o'clock (even though the typical viewer's eye initially focuses on the eleven o'clock position). If the variables of size, value, and texture reinforce each other, readers easily order and quantify the information in the pie chart. For example, in Figure 5.28, the biggest wedges of the pie are also the darkest wedges: therefore, the ordered variable of value reinforces the ordered and proportional variable of size. In Figure 5.29, however, there is no correspondence between the size and value of the wedges, and the mixed message thus impairs the reader's comprehension of the illustration. If the wedges of a pie are approximately the same size, readers find it difficult to discern their relationship; in this situation, the position and value of the wedges constitute the only visual signals regarding the hierarchy of the pieces. Therefore, it is critical that the pie chart display traditional ordering of the wedges with a corresponding gradation of value.

Organizational Charts

Organizational charts illustrate the hierarchical arrangement of personnel and departments, thereby clarifying lines of authority and responsibility. A series of rectangles are arranged in the shape of a pyramid; the narrowest point at

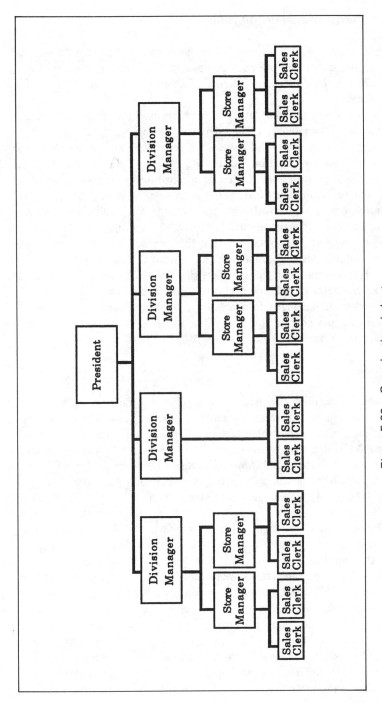

Figure 5.30. Organizational chart.

the top displays the highest positions and the base displays the lowest positions within the organization. The presence or absence of connecting lines between rectangles indicates the presence or absence of a direct relationship between the represented divisions.

Each row identifies a different level within an organization; distance from the top or bottom of the pyramid is a visual signal of the importance of the position within the organization. To avoid misleading readers regarding the status of individuals within an organization, editors are careful to display positions of equal rank in the same row, even if there is no position in the row or rows immediately above or below (see Figure 5.30). Similarly, the size of the rectangles is either uniform or proportional with the status of the position within the organization. Lines of different texture (e.g., dotted lines or dashed lines) indicate special or indirect relationships inside the organization or between the organization and outside individuals or agencies (e.g., lawyers, distributors, advertisers). In organizational charts, selectivity and order are communicated by the retinal variables of value and texture; that is, because of the gradually increasing number of rectangles in successive rows across the page, the visual space surrounding the top of the pyramid is lighter and less dense than the available space at the bottom.

Flow Charts

A flow chart illustrates the steps in a process or procedure, with arrows indicating the sequence or direction of activity. In this type of figure, different shapes (e.g., rectangles, circles, diamonds) and arrows (e.g., solid lines, dotted lines, dashed lines) are used systematically to represent different operations. The steps are labeled and arranged from left to right in order to facilitate reading, corresponding to the way the eye moves as it examines an illustration. For example, in Figure 5.31, the sequence of steps has been designed so that the initial activity appears on the upper left side of the flow chart, with subsequent steps positioned to the lower right. This top-left to bottom-right staircase suggests decreasing complexity or difficulty, and a bottom-left to top-right progression implies the opposite.

Figure 5.32, however, illustrates how reading is impaired by an inconsistent positioning of steps. Though the horizontal ordering is sequential, the vertical positioning is arbitrary and therefore disorienting.

In addition, editors design flow charts so that the left to right and top to bottom movement is reinforced by the retinal variables. For example, the unordered and associative variable of shape is necessary if the steps of a process are of different kinds but are of equal importance. On the other hand, if various steps differ also in their importance, the ordered variable of texture is required. If the arrows differ in value or texture (e.g., solid lines for required steps versus

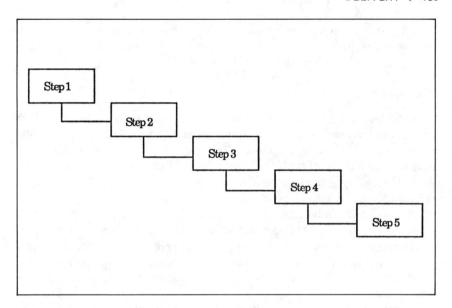

Figure 5.31. Flow chart visually emphasizing simplicity of procedure.

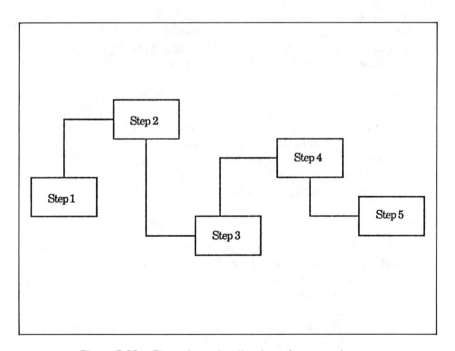

Figure 5.32. Flow chart visually obscuring procedure.

dotted lines for optional steps; plain lines for routine steps versus bold lines for emergency steps), readers easily associate related steps and focus on specific steps or kinds of steps readily.

Diagrams

A diagram is a representational and proportional sketch or outline which provides an overview of a subject by identifying its parts and illustrating their relationship. In designing diagrams, editors decide on the point of view (i.e., internal, external, or exploded) and on the angle of vision (i.e., top, bottom, front, back, side, or three-dimensional perspective) which display or emphasize the details of the subject pertinent to the communicative aim and audience of the discourse. Ordinarily, only the information necessary to the viewer's understanding is illustrated and distracting details are omitted. For example, a diagram of a typewriter designed for typists is likely to be a top angle, external view, emphasizing the keys of the keyboard; designed for typewriter repairers, the diagram is likely to be a three-dimensional internal view, focusing on the inner mechanisms.

In directing the viewer's attention to the important characteristics of the subject, a diagram exploits the retinal variables of size, value, texture, and color. For example, the viewer's perspective on the numeric keys of a typewriter keyboard might be guided by magnifying them, making them lighter or darker than the remaining keys, giving them a finer or coarser grain, or assigning them a "hot" advancing color such as red and the remaining keys a "cool" receding color such as green.

Important also to the effectiveness of a diagram is the labeling of its various parts. The traditional left-to-right motion of the reader's or viewer's eye is here complicated by the diagram's combination of visual and verbal information, and especially by their relative positions. With labels surrounding the subject, for example, the eye focuses initially on the subject, moves to the upper left portion of the diagram, and proceeds in a clockwise direction, beginning with the top left label (approximately the eleven o'clock position) (see Figure 5.33).

Drawings

A drawing is a depiction of people or objects focusing on the appearance of the subject. Similar to diagrams, drawings easily omit inappropriate or distracting details and focus the viewer's attention through manipulation of the retinal variables. A drawing, however, is as realistic or unrealistic as is appropriate to the communicative aim and audience of the discourse (see Figures 5.34 and 5.35). For example, editorial cartoonists often exaggerate the physical characteristics of political officials in order to amuse the voting public, whereas a police artist aims for a realistic representation.

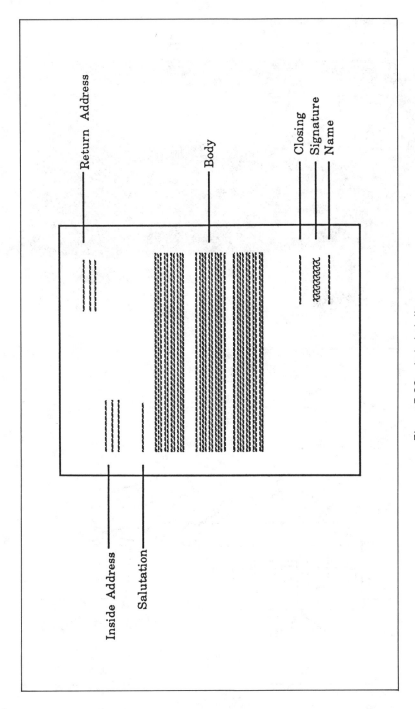

Figure 5.33. Labeled diagram.

Figure 5.34. Realistic drawing.

Figure 5.35. Less realistic drawing.

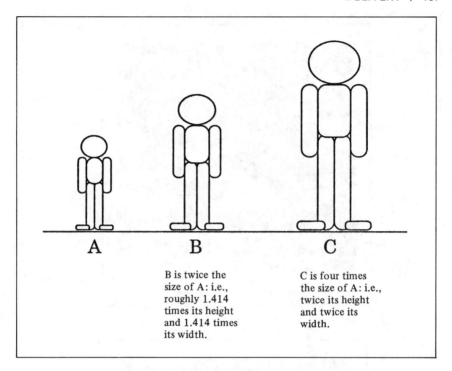

B is twice the
size of A: i.e.,
roughly 1.414
times its height
and 1.414 times
its width.

C is four times
the size of A: i.e.,
twice its height
and twice its
width.

Figure 5.36. Proportionally sized symbols.

Pictographs

Pictographs combine the characteristics of pictorial and non-pictorial illustrations to reinforce meaning and improve the memorability of the information. Like graphs and charts, pictographs communicate a change of quantity over time or the condition of a subject at a given point in time. Like diagrams and drawings, pictographs communicate information through representational illustrations. For example, a pie chart might easily illustrate the major divisions of a typical person's entertainment dollar: however, a dollar bill instead of a circle and visual symbols (e.g., pictures of a book, television, movie camera) instead of verbal labels exploit the viewer's orientation to the pictorial.

Similarly, to illustrate population changes over a 5-year period, editors might choose a traditional line graph; also possible, however, is a pictograph using stick people to symbolize a given population size and a doubling of the number of stick people to signify a doubling of the population. A doubling of the size of the graph symbol is often deceptive because a magnification of height also yields a proportional magnification of width: a symbol twice the size thus occupies

The original photograph includes distracting details.

Cropping L's allow the editor to identify and size the desirable area of the original.

Figure 5.37. Cropping a photograph.

Marks in the border indicate the areas of the photograph to be cropped.

The cropped photograph can be used as is or enlarged or reduced proportionally.

Figure 5.37. Cropping a photograph (cont'd).

four times the space. A graphic symbol which genuinely occupies only twice the space never looks twice the size (see Figure 5.36).

Photographs

A photograph is a realistic pictorial illustration, replicating on film the appearance of people and objects. To reinforce this realism, editors ordinarily choose candid photographs with active subjects or implied motion over posed photographs with passive or static subjects. The realism of photographs also heightens the characteristics associated with pictorial illustrations: that is, the viewer's eye readily focuses on photographs, especially photographs of human beings, especially their faces, especially their eyes [10, pp. 279-280]. If the subject of the photograph is looking to the right, the viewer also looks to the right: if the subject is looking left, or up, or down, the viewer does likewise [10, pp. 280-281].

Also directing the viewer's perception of photographs are the retinal variables. Though ordinarily photographs are rectangular, for example, it is possible to have circles, ovals, and even silhouettes: the special shapes yield distinctive and easily associated pictures. Similarly, the majority of photographs are horizontally and vertically oriented: a diagonal orientation therefore solicits the viewer's special attention. Full color intensifies photographic realism, as does the fine texture of a crisp focus: the photograph itself is invisible and the viewer sees only the subject which it displays. Black and white or a coarse and grainy texture, however, reminds the viewer that the photograph is only a photograph, only a replica of reality. Value is significant because photographs display a continuum of values between black and white, and the viewer especially notices the polarities of this continuum: areas of black on white or white on black. And size is important because the size of a photographic subject differs according to its proximity to the camera. Size is also a proportional variable with its quantitative and qualitative significance linked: thus the importance of a photographic subject is perceived as increasing or decreasing with proximity to the camera. In a photograph or grouping of photographs, therefore, important subjects are closer to the camera and thus bigger.

A photograph, however, often has visual details without relevance to the subject of the discourse. This is because it is impossible to design a photograph as easily as it is a diagram or drawing. Though the graphic artist is given creative license with which to picture a subject, the photographer is always required to negotiate the restrictions of reality: for example, the subject who never smiles, the picture hanging crooked on the wall, the reflection of light in a mirror or window, the empty chairs at the important meeting, the man's plaid suit beside the woman's striped dress.

Similarly, the implied notion of the subjects within a photograph might be distracting. For example, because the viewer's eye moves left to right across the photograph, the left side is associated with the past and the right side with the future. A subject's motion within a photograph is usually perceived to be motion from left to right. A figure walking to the right side of a photograph seems to be walking forward, but a figure walking to the left side appears to be walking backward. A figure looking to the left seems to be turning to the right, turning to face the viewer; a figure looking to the right also seems to be turning to the right, and thus to have previously faced the viewer.

It is possible to adjust photographs, however. Editors often minimize distracting detail, for example, by cropping or cutting a photograph to eliminate unnecessary or undesirable areas (see Figure 5.37). A photograph is flopped to allow a subject originally looking to the left to face the right, or vice versa (though flopping is impractical if there is writing within the photograph). Or editors emphasize the equal importance of subjects within a series of photographs by cropping and enlarging or reducing the cropped photographs to give the subjects equal size (though enlarging a photograph excessively yields a less crisp image and thus modifies the variable of texture, while reducing a photograph eliminates white space and thereby changes its value).

Page Design

Page design is the positioning of verbal and visual information within a horizontal and vertical space. The objective is to capitalize on the aesthetics of the typography and illustrations and thus intensify the rhetorical power of the discourse.

In designing a page, the editor typically observes several basic principles of positioning: the reader's eye moves left to right and top to bottom, but focusing on illustrations before typography [11, p. 35]. In a two-page spread of a book or magazine, the eye crosses from the left (or verso) page to the right (or recto) page [11, p. 46]. Of all illustrations, readers notice figures before tables, preferring pictorial figures to non-pictorial figures. Of all typography, big and bold type dominates small and plain. White space is equally important: it organizes and unifies the page, divides blocks of discourse, implies elegance, guides the eye through the page, and links neighboring pages.

The editor also has to consider the reading process itself. The ideal page design satisfies a reader's every reading of a discourse. In thumbing through a magazine, for example, the reader focuses on the top right quarter of the recto page and will stop to examine the entire page only if that quarter offers visual gratification. The editor might position a picture here because this is likely to stop the reader's eye. In the subsequent examination of the page, however, the eye moves from top to bottom or left to right: that is, from the top right corner of the page to the bottom right quarter and off the page or from the top right quarter to right off the page. If the editor chooses a picture of a person looking

Figure 5.38. Sample page grids.

to the left, however, this is likely to stop the reader on that page and direct the eye to the inside quarters of the recto page and on to the verso page.

Given the basic principles of positioning and a sensitivity to the process of reading itself, the editor has to determine the basic page grid, specifically the page size, the size and number of columns, and the size of margins and gutters (i.e., the white space between columns) (see Figure 5.38). With serial publications especially, however, the page grid is often prescribed by the publishing organization or by tradition and the editor is required to adjust the verbal and visual display of information to this established grid.

Page size varies considerably. Letter size (i.e., 8.5 X 11 inches) is typical of magazines, newsletters, flyers, bifold booklets, and trifold brochures, whereas legal size (i.e., 8.5 X 14 inches) is often used for newsletters, flyers, and quadrifold brochures. Common book size is 6 X 9 inches.

Figure 5.39. Publication with short page.

All pages of a publication are normally the same size, but two exceptions have wide currency: the narrow page and the fold-out page. The narrow page only has to be one or two inches narrower: if readers riffle the pages of the publication, their fingers always miss the narrow page: as a consequence, the riffling stops and the publication opens at the narrow page (see Figure 5.39). Especially important verbal or visual information is thus often given on this and neighboring pages. The fold-out page, on the other hand, is normally a double-wide page used to display illustrations or a glossary of technical

Figure 5.40. Publication with fold-out page.

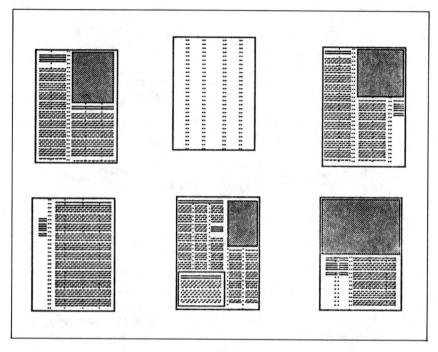

Figure 5.41. Variations of a five-column page grid.

terminology. This page unfolds to lie either to the right of the recto pages or to the left of the verso pages and is therefore available for readers to examine as necessary during their reading of the publication (see Figure 5.40).

The number and width of columns differ with the size of the page. Letter-size pages usually have one, two, or three columns, with four or five columns possible. Column width is measured in picas and is often equal for all columns on the grid: however, such regularity is unnecessary. A five-column letter-size grid, for example, allows considerable variation (see Figure 5.41). Similarly, the space given to margins and gutters differs according to page size, with a letter-size page typically getting margins of 3 picas on either side and 4.5 picas on top and bottom. Variation is possible: for example, omitting the margins and "bleeding" a photograph to give the feeling that it continues off the page. Gutter size for a two-column grid is ordinarily 2 picas, and for a three-column grid is 1.5 picas.

Also important to page design is the editor's decision on using boxes and rules (i.e., horizontal or vertical lines reinforcing the visual definition of margins, columns, and blocks of discourse). Their omission exploits the white spaces of the page. Their inclusion offers a variety of design choices: for example, rules might be thick or thin, plain or embroidered, and boxes come filled and un-filled, with squared or rounded corners.

Obviously, the retinal variables differ according to the page design. Size is perceived, for example, as the width of columns: a page of wide columns seems superior to a page of narrow columns. Value and texture differ according to the distribution of typography and illustrations: a page with a strict three columns of type is a homogeneous grey whereas a page with three columns of type, bold headings, and several photographs has complexity and density. And because page design exploits the ordered variables of size, value, and texture, it is important that editors design pages with sensitivity to the position that a given page has within the hierarchical series of neighboring pages. The editor never designs a single page because the design of page 1 has to guide the eye to page 2 and page 2 to page 3. And if page 1 visually dominates page 2, it is necessary to the ordering of the pages that page 2 visually dominate page 3.

Similarity of page design, however, elicits visual association. Editors thus unify a publication by using common design characteristics: for example, a thin horizontal rule across the top of each page or a special color for all headings. Pages carrying equivalent categories of information or covering the same subject might display additional design similarities: for example, columns of equal number and width or headings of identical style and alignment.

Production

Though verbal and visual information might occur strictly as a series of elec-tronic images on a video display screen, the majority of written discourse is committed to paper. And the production processes of printing, folding, and binding emphasize the physical dimension of the canon of delivery.

Printing

The traditional printing press is a machine which, like a typewriter, uses inked relief images. Instead of striking paper with individual letters the way a typewriter does, however, the image of a full page is pressed on to the paper. Originally, each page required individual mechanical preparation of its verbal and visual display: a compositor would arrange the various pieces of type, and engravers would develop etchings of the illustrations. With technological inno-vations, different techniques have evolved which simplify the preparation of visual and verbal information, with two photographic processes prevailing: xerography and offset lithography.

Xerography or photocopying is a dry process, using a resinous powder and electrostatic forces as opposed to ink and direct mechanical pressure. On a photographic plate, a positively charged image of the original is composed and negatively charged powder is applied. As positively charged paper is passed over the image, the negatively charged powder affixes itself to the paper. Simultaneously, electrical melting of the powder allows the paper to absorb the image, yielding a xerographic copy of the original. Xerography is the printing process of various commercial copy services: it requires the editor's preparation of a perfect or "camera" copy of the original.

In offset lithography or offset printing, a chemical coating on a flexible photographic plate allows the image of the original to receive ink. During the printing process, the photographic plate is given continuous applications of ink and water: the ink affixes to the image, while the water washes the ink off the spaces surrounding the image. This printing process also requires a press with three major cylinders: a photographic plate cylinder, blanket cylinder, and impression cylinder. The blanket cylinder receives the inked image off the photographic plate and transfers this image to paper passing between the blanket cylinder and the impression cylinder. Offset lithography is the process characteristic of commercial printing services and requires the preparation of a camera copy of the original either by the editor or a compositor.

Xerography and offset lithography do a superior job of copying original black and white images (e.g., typography). Their capacity for copying the continuous values between black and white as well as for copying color, however, is limited. For example, in order to use photographs, either printing process must substitute black and white dots for the continuous values or tones of photographs. This is accomplished by photographing the original photograph through a screen, a process called halftone reproduction. Light reflected from the original photograph, passes through the holes of the screen, and strikes the film of the new photograph as a series of dots. The white areas of the original photograph reflect light, the black areas absorb it, and the various intermediate areas reflect and absorb light to differing degrees according to their value. Thus the intensity of the reflected light passing through the screen and striking the film differs, and the resulting dots on the film differ in their size and spacing. (Obviously, a black and white original yields a crisper image.) The coarseness of the screen used for halftone reproduction also varies, with newspapers typically using screens of 85 to 100 intersecting lines per inch (i.e., 7225 to 10,000 dots per square inch) and magazines often using screens of 120 to 133 lines per inch (i.e., 14,400 to 17,689 dots per square inch). The finer the screen, the more like the original photograph is the halftone reproduction. This is because the human eye blends the individual dots and focuses on the image thus composed: a mix of black and white dots, as a consequence, looks grey. The smaller the dots and the denser their spacing, the easier is this visual blending.

A second way of substituting black and white dots for the continuous values of photographs and similar illustrations is a computerized conversion technique called digitizing. A computerized scanner examines each point of the original image and replicates the image with a series of equally sized and variously spaced dots.

Introducing color is similarly complex. Typically, xerography and offset lithography use black ink. Full color requires a technique called four-color process or color separation. The original image is digitized or photographed through filters and screens to produce a photographic plate for each of the four colors composing the original (i.e., yellow, red, blue, and black). Using the corresponding four colors of ink, the printing process yields a series of overlapping dots which the eye blends to perceive full color.

It is also possible to introduce limited color, reinforcing or replacing black with a single color or with several colors. Each additional color of ink, however, requires its individual photographic plate or pass through the xerographic copier or lithographic press.

In addition, screening of ink allows a variety of lighter values of a single color, thus essentially adding white to the color. For example, a 10 percent screen of red allows only 10 percent of the red ink through: the human eye blends the red dots with the surrounding white space to perceive a delicate pink. Combining screens of black with screens of color yields a variety of darker values of that color, essentially adding black to the color. A screen of 50 percent black and 70 percent red thus produces a vigorous maroon. Screening gives the impression of additional colors without the associated costs and offers the editor a variety of design choices: for example, a black diagram laid on a 20 percent screen of color gives the figure dimension and emphasis. The hierarchy of screens (10 percent to 100 percent) also allows the visual ordering of information, while special screens (e.g., using horizontal lines or concentric circles) offer distinctive textures.

Paper

The editor's choice of paper is often critical to the rhetorical power of written discourse, clarifying or obscuring the typography, illustrations, and page design. The variety of papers is impressive, with important differences of composition, durability, grain, kind, finish, weight, bulk, and opacity.

Paper is a blend of raw ingredients, typically wood and cotton fibers. Wood fiber, though inexpensive, is brittle and thus papers with a high wood fiber composition (e.g., newspaper) have a low durability. Papers with a high cotton fiber composition (e.g., bond writing paper) have a high durability and a high cost. Grain is the direction of the various fibers, important only because folding and cutting is easiest along the grain.

Usage identifies the different kinds of paper (e.g., bond writing paper, book paper, cover paper). Basis weight designates the weight of 500 sheets of the basic size of a paper, with this size differing according to the kind of paper. Bond has

Table 5.1. Equivalencies of Common Basis Weights

Bond	Book	Cover
13	–	–
16	40	–
20	50	–
24	60	–
–	70	–
–	80	–
–	100	–
–	–	60
–	–	65
–	–	80
–	–	90

a basic size of 17 X 22 inches (yielding four 8.5 X 11 inch pages), book has a basis of 25 X 38 inches, and cover paper has a basis of 20 X 26 inches. Because of this size disparity, papers of equal weight have different basis weight designations (see Table 5.1). In addition to its basic size, each kind of paper is available in a variety of common or standard sizes:

bond paper: 8.5X11, 8.5X14, 11X17, 17X28, 19X24, 19X28, 22X34, and 34X44 inches;
book paper: 17.5X22.5, 19X25, 23X29, 23X35, 35X45, 38X40, 50X76 inches;
cover paper: 23X35, 25X38, 26X40, and 35X45 inches.

The weight of a specific standard size of paper is given as the M weight (i.e., the weight of 1000 sheets). Bond and book paper are also available on rolls according to gross weight.

Paper is also either coated or uncoated. Coatings give paper various degrees of dull or glossy finish. Ink sits on the chemical coating and is distributed equally deep across a given image. The entire image thus absorbs light uniformly, and typographical or illustrative detail looks crisp. Ordinarily, the glossier the finish, the more expensive it is. Glossy finishes also reflect more light, reducing readability [8, pp. 155-159] but intensifying the brilliance of colors.

Uncoated papers come in a variety of rough and smooth finishes. Without a coating, paper absorbs ink; and the rougher the finish, the more irregular is this absorption and the more uneven the resulting image. Smoothing is accomplished through calendering, a mechanical process of pressing the paper through rollers. The more calendering that paper receives, the smoother and more expensive it is.

Bulk is the thickness of the paper, usually measured as pages per inch. The heavier and rougher a paper is, the bulkier it is. Bulk often determines the kind of binding a publication is given, or vice versa.

Opacity is the degree to which ink on a page is visible on the reverse side of the page. This is a function of bulk and ink absorption: that is, either the eye sees through the paper to the reverse side, or the ink on the reverse side comes through the paper to the visible side. The thicker that coated paper is, or the thicker and smoother uncoated paper is, the more opaque it is.

Obviously, the characteristics of paper exploit tactile as well as retinal variables. The various finishes of paper differ to the touch and to the eye. And because tactile texture reinforces visual texture, readers easily perceive that papers of similar finish carry associated information. Editors thus might unify a publication by using the same paper for all pages or might divide a publication by using a different paper to characterize each division and communicate the hierarchy of the divisions through a corresponding ordering of the weights and finishes of the different papers.

Folding and Binding

If multiple pages of a publication are printed on the same side of a single sheet of paper, folding of the paper is required. In order for the folded pages to occur in numerical order, the editor or compositor appropriately positions the pages on the camera copy (see Figure 5.42). The folded paper, called a signature, is trimmed if necessary. (Thick paper is often scored or grooved prior to folding.)

Equally critical to the delivery of written discourse is the binding of the pages. Ideally, a binding is appropriate for the manner and frequency of reading that the publication is likely to receive. For example, a book designed for studious examination requires a binding that allows the book to lie open on a desk, whereas a book which receives only a single quick reading deserves a simpler binding. And the editor has a wide variety of bindings among which to choose.

Zero Binding

This is the binding characteristic of newspapers and circulars: it is binding by folding along the gutter between the recto and verso pages. Edges of the three

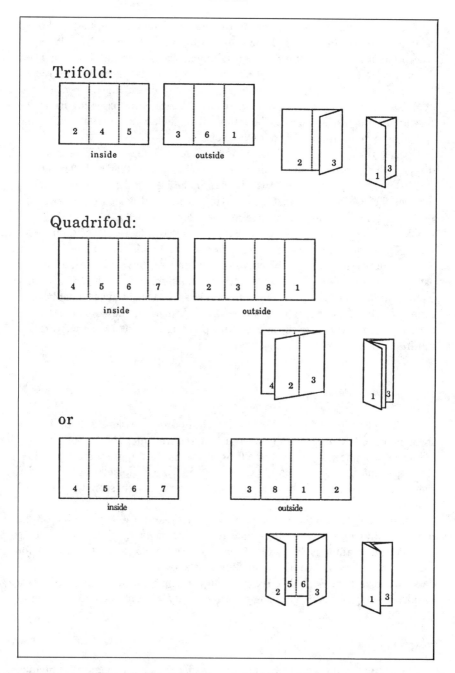

Figure 5.42. Imposition and folding of brochure.

remaining sides are trimmed. The cover requires no special paper. Though this binding allows the publication to open a full 360 degrees, it is as transitory as it is inexpensive: often the publication is disjoined and its pages variously distributed. Obviously, this binding is suitable only for publications of limited thickness (approximately one-half inch).

Saddle-wire Binding

This is the inexpensive binding of magazines and pamphlets. It is identical to the zero binding, but with the sheets or signatures stapled together through the gutter fold. Trimming of the remaining three sides is typical, and the cover is often of the same weight and finish of paper. Publications open 360 degrees, but their integrity is preserved.

Side-wire Binding

This binding is often used with pages trimmed on all sides. The individual sheets are simply collated, stacked, and stapled together along the left margin, depriving the publication of the ability to open even 180 degrees. Requiring no special cover and limited to publications of approximately one-half inch thickness, this process is quick and inexpensive. It also has good durability.

Post Binding

Similar to side-wire binding, post binding uses two or three holes punched along the trimmed left margin of the publication, fastening the individual sheets together with metal posts inserted through the holes. No special cover is necessary. Post binding is inexpensive and sacrifices permanency and the ability to open 180 degrees for the capacity to add or subtract pages as desired.

Press Binding

With a press binding, the individual sheets of a publication are collated, stacked, and then pressed together between two metal strips along the trimmed left margin. The cover is ordinarily a heavier weight of paper. Publications thus have a more attractive and expensive binding, but still no ability to open 180 degrees.

Spiral Binding

This is the binding characteristic of notebooks. A spiral binding has a series of holes, along the left or top margin, through which a single wire spirals. More expensive, attractive, and durable, this binding typically uses a heavier weight of paper as the cover and allows the publication to open 360 degrees while maintaining the ordering of the pages. It is also suitable for thicker publications (approximately one inch).

Comb Binding

Similar to spiral binding is a comb binding. A strip of curled plastic or metal teeth pierces a corresponding series of holes along the trimmed left margin of the publication, binding the individual sheets. The cover is usually a heavier weight of paper. Suitable for publications as thick as one inch, comb bindings allow publications to open 360 degrees with the ordering of pages preserved. In addition, it is possible to open a comb binding in order to insert or delete pages. Wire combs have high durability, but plastic are less expensive.

Ring Binding

With this binding, two or three metal or plastic rings (attached either to a soft cover of heavy paper or plastic or to a hard cover of vinyl- or cloth-covered cardboard) are inserted through corresponding holes punched along the trimmed left margin of the publication. The cost and durability of this binding differ according to the quality of the rings and cover: metal rings and a hard cover usually prove more expensive, offering better and longer protection to the pages of the publication. Ring binders open 180 degrees, allow the easiest possible insertion and deletion of pages, and suit publications as thick as three inches.

Perfect Binding

This is the binding characteristic of paperback books. The signatures of the book are collated and stacked; adhesive is then applied to the spine (i.e., the side of the stacked signatures that is adjacent to the left margin) and a heavy paper cover is affixed at the spine. Signatures are trimmed either before or after binding to the cover. Publications with perfect binding come as thick as three inches, but have limited capacity to open 180 degrees because this damages the binding. Cost and durability are low.

Sewn Binding

In this more expensive and durable binding, untrimmed signatures are sewn together along the spine (with a saddle stitch through each signature or a side stitch through all signatures). If a soft cover is to be used, adhesive is applied to the spine and the heavy paper cover is affixed. Pages might be trimmed before or after application of the cover. If a hard cover is desired, heavier weight end papers are sewn to the signatures, the signatures and end papers are trimmed, adhesive is applied to the end papers, and the cover is then affixed. Sewn bindings allow publications to open 180 degrees and are suitable for even the thickest of publications.

	Printing	Paper	Folding/ Binding	Typography	Illustrations	Page Design
Aim						
Audience						
Verbal Information						
Visual Information						

Figure 5.43. Delivery matrix.

Editing for Artistry

In editing for artistry, the editor initially reviews the communicative aim and audience as well as the verbal and visual information of the discourse because these factors solicit distinct and often competing delivery specifications. Using the delivery matrix (see Figure 5.43) as a guide, the editor chooses the printing process, paper, folding and binding, typography, illustrations, and page design. Consider, for example, a user's manual:

Aim: The aim of the discourse is to inform and instruct: this aim stipulates either a xerographic or lithographic printing process; a heavyweight paper, possibly coated for durability, of small size to group information and limit the number of instructions per page; and a spiral or comb binding to allow the manual to open a full 360 degrees and fully display a single page of instructions. No special folding is required. The instructive and informative aim of the user's manual solicits variations of size, style, and color of type to identify different blocks of discourse (e.g., instructions, explanations, and warnings). Illustrations adopt the user's point of view and display only the detail necessary to the user's training. Page design allows substantial white space, positions information within a single column to allow the easiest possible left to right and top to bottom reading, and limits typography and illustrations to minimize the user's dismay or panic.

Audience: If the audience is 10,000 college students, this specifies a lithographic printing to produce the required volume quickly and economically; an inexpensive, but heavyweight uncoated paper, of small size to isolate instructions on a given operation; a spiral or comb binding to open a full 360 degrees and thus direct the reader's attention to the instructions on a single page and occupy less space on a desk or lap. No special folding is required. An audience of college students allows a typesize of 10 points, with bigger sizes for headings and warnings. Tolerance for sans serif typefaces might also be higher. Illustrations might depict users as college age. No special design of pages is necessary.

Verbal Information: If the user's manual is verbally oriented, either xerography or offset lithography is satisfactory; an uncoated paper with a smooth finish is desirable as this offers a crisp letter image, minimizing reflection and improving readability. No special folding or binding is necessary. If the manual has brief instructions and explanations, a sans serif typeface is judicious. Detailed instructions and paragraphs of explanation, however, require a serif design; narrow columns to restrict line length and a ragged right margin might also improve readability. In addition, a verbal orientation leaves the page a homogeneous grey: as a consequence, illustrations might be designed with either color or crisp blacks and whites and pages given liberal white space. Similarly, type might be varied in size and style to bring diversity of value and texture to the page.

Visual Information: If the manual requires numerous diagrams and photographs, offset lithography is likely to offer superior quality and coated paper is desirable for clarity and brilliance. No special folding or binding is necessary. Visually oriented illustrations such as diagrams and photographs prove distinctive in value and texture from the surrounding typography: as a consequence, no change of typeface is necessary for their labels and captions (as is often required with verbally oriented illustrations such as tables). Diagrams and photographs also solicit the user's initial attention (especially if designed to include human beings); and their position on the page above or to the left of the typographical display encourages reading of the directions as well as viewing of the instructive figures.

This initial level of analysis shows that the user's manual merits a lithographic printing, a small size of paper, and a spiral or comb binding. Neither coated nor uncoated paper, however, is clearly indicated. The editor therefore has to judge: a heavyweight uncoated paper with a smooth finish satisfies the stipulations of the audience and verbal information; it also offers approximately the clarity specified by the visual information as well as the durability required by the discourse aim. Typographical display has a basic size of 9 or 10 points, with variations of size and style for headings and warnings. If the discourse is verbally oriented, a serif typeface is fitting; if visually oriented, a sans serif design. Line length is limited, with a ragged right margin. Color or crisp black and white illustrations depict users as college students and show only the detail which users require. The page is designed as a single column with a generous use of white space and illustrations above and to the left of verbal instructions.

It is also critical that the editor assess the felicity of the delivery choices. For example, if the editor decides on a spiral or comb binding, as much as a half inch along the left margin of the recto pages and the right margin of the verso pages is dedicated to the binding. The editor, as a consequence, has to design the page to suit the binding, and vice versa. Similarly, a spiral or comb binding proscribes typography or illustrations that cross the binding.

PRACTICE

The canon of delivery is obviously complex: the editor is asked to consider the aim, audience, and verbal and visual information of the discourse, to assess their influence on the choice of printing process, paper, folding and binding, typography, illustrations, and page design, and by weighing this multiplicity of specifications, to determine a physical presentation of artistry and eloquence. It is thus crucial that rhetorical theory and empirical research on discourse design inform the editor's delivery decisions.

The following samples of technical, news, and promotional publications illustrate the application of the Editor's Delivery Inventory (see Figure 5.44), a practical guide through the complexities of editing for artistry. In addition, paired editing symbols indicate to a compositor the typographical design, size, and style of various blocks of verbal discourse as well as the captions and labels of illustrations.

A Technical Publication

This sample is from a research report intended for publication in a professional journal (see Figure 5.45). The accompanying matrix (see Figure 5.46) displays the editor's choices regarding delivery.

Typography

1. What are the characteristics of the basic type design? What retinal variations of design occur? What is their significance?
The basic type design is serif, with average x-height, fairly narrow counters, average ascenders and descenders, obvious variation between thicks and thins, and clear vertical stress. This is a conventional type design, suitable for this verbally oriented document. The same design (and thus the same texture) is maintained throughout, keeping the various blocks of information clearly associated.

Typography

1. What are the characteristics of the basic type design (i.e., serif/sans serif, x-height, counters, ascenders and descenders, thicks and thins, vertical stress)? What retinal variations of design occur? What is their significance (associative, selective, ordered)?
2. What is the basic point size of type? What retinal variations of size occur? What is their significance (selective, ordered, proportional)?
3. What is the basic style of type (i.e., bold, italic, underlined, outline, shadow, positive/negative images, chromatic/achromatic, upper/lower case)? What retinal variations of style occur? What is their significance (associative, selective, ordered, proportional)?
4. What is the basic horizontal and vertical spacing (i.e. line length, leading, alignment)? What retinal variations of spacing occur? What is their significance (associative, selective, ordered, proportional)?

Illustrations

Tables

1. What are the typographical characteristics of each table (i.e., design, size, style, and spacing)? What retinal variations of design, size, style, and spacing occur? What is their significance (associative, selective, ordered, proportional)?
2. What are the illustrative characteristics of each table (e.g., boxing, color, screens)? What retinal variations of the illustrative characteristics occur? What is the significance of the retinal variations (associative, selective, ordered, proportional)?

Figures

1. What are the illustrative characteristics of each figure (i.e., pictorial/non-pictorial)? What retinal variations of the illustrative characteristics occur? What is the significance of the retinal variations (associative, selective, ordered, proportional)?
2. What are the typographical characteristics of each figure (i.e., design, size, style, and spacing)? What retinal variations of design, size, style, and spacing occur? What is their significance (associative, selective, ordered, proportional)?
3. Do the illustrative and typographical characteristics of each figure communicate or reinforce a single and unified meaning?
4. Does each figure encourage viewing as opposed to reading? How is this achieved?

Page Design

1. What is the basic page grid? What retinal variations of this page grid occur (e.g., column number, column width, margin size)? What is the significance of the retinal variations (associative, selective, ordered, proportional)?
2. Which pages of the publication deserve the reader's initial attention? the reader's subsequent attention? Why? Do these pages solicit this attention? How?
3. Which illustrations on each page deserve the reader's initial attention? the reader's subsequent attention? Why? Do these illustrations solicit this attention? How?
4. Which blocks of typography on each page deserve the reader's initial attention? the reader's subsequent attention? Why? Do these blocks of typography solicit this attention? How?

Production

1. Does the printing process harmonize with the typography, illustrations, and page design?
2. Does the paper harmonize with the typography, illustrations, and page design?
3. Does the folding/binding process harmonize with the typography, illustrations, and page design?

Figure 5.44. Editor's delivery inventory.

Times 10/12

(bf)
(fl) (Ital)
(Ital)

Evaluation   page 15

]Results and Discussion[
Writing Apprehension

Table 1 presents the results of the 2 two-tailed $\underline{t}$-
tests for the changes in response to the Daly-Miller
Writing Apprehension Test (1975).

[Insert Table 1 here]

Curiously, students in both the control and the experimental groups showed significant increases in apprehen-
sion across the semester ($\underline{t}$ = -2.21, $\underline{t}$ = -2.16, $\underline{p}$<.05).
The small but significant increases in apprehension were
clearly not expected, and, perhaps equally important, did
not distinguish between the control and experimental
group.

To test for the possibility that the Daly-Miller,
as a whole, was not sensitive enough to pick up differences in students' attitudes toward evaluation of their
writing, a subscale of ten items was created from that
test. These ten items—1, 2, 4, 6, 12, 18, 22, and 25—all
probe students' attitudes about having others read their
writing and about having their essays evaluated. Table 2
presents the results.

[Insert Table 2 here]

Although the control group did not show significant
decreases on these ten items ($\underline{t}$ = 0.86, $\underline{p}$>.05), the experimental group improved significantly ($\underline{t}$ = 2.68,
$\underline{p}$<.01). Student writers in the experimental group responded positively to the one-to-one conferences in which
they discussed their writing and suggestions for guided
revision with their instructors. In addition, these
Student writers became more comfortable and confident
about the evaluation process in the experimental group
when their essays were rated the same by two outside
readers. The rater agreement and guidelines for revision

Figure 5.45. Editing a technical publication for artistry.

Evaluation   page 16

put these student writers more at ease about writing for
other readers and submitting essays for evaluation.

    Two interesting questions emerge from the subscale
results, where students' overall apprehension increased
but their apprehension about evaluation decreased: Is
writing apprehension as influential and important an
entity as the Daly-Miller assumes it is? And how sensitive is this test as an indicator of apprehension?

(fl) (ital)

Writing Quality

    Two different procedures were used for determining
writing quality in the two groups. Control group essays
were graded in the traditional manner (A, B, C, etc.);
experimental group essays were evaluated holistically on
a 0-100 scale. This difference coupled with the fact
that different topics for the expressive, referential,
and persuasive essays were used to measure pre- and post-
course writing quality make it impossible to compare the
two groups directly. Nevertheless, improvement over the
semester can be at least estimated by comparing grades on
an early and later paper for the control group and by
comparing holistic scores of an early and a later paper
for the experimental group.

    In the first case, the results seemed valid in
light of the fact that the instructors' grades were
purely dependent on the perceived quality of the writing
(i.e., not influenced by pedagogical considerations) and
the writing tasks chosen from the beginning and end of
the semester made roughly the same demands on the student
writers. In the second case, the results seemed valid in
light of the fact that the raters evaluated the pre- and
post-essays on the same scale and the writing tasks were
equivalent.

    Table 3 shows an estimate of the improvement in
writing quality over the semester based on the comparison
of early and later papers described above. Given the
validity of the results, the data suggest that both
groups improved significantly in writing quality.

Figure 5.45.   Editing a technical publication for artistry (cont'd).

Evaluation   page 17

[Insert Table 3 here]

The control group showed some increase in writing quality
(ital) from the expressive essay to the persuasive essay ($\underline{t}$ = -
(ital) 0.42, $\underline{p}$<.01). However, the experimental group made
(ital) extraordinary progress from essay 1 to essay 5 ($\underline{t}$ = -
(ital) 3.01, $\underline{p}$<.01). Again, though the grades of students whose
work had been evaluated traditionally steadily increased,
their progress was not commensurate with the increase in
quality of those students whose writing had been evaluated both by summative and formative techniques. The
guided revision and one-to-one conferencing seemed to
increase the writing abilities of students significantly.

To measure the reliability of raters of the experimental group's essays, a Spearman's Rho (i.e., a type of
correlation between rank order data) was used. The correlation coefficients for each of the five essays were
determined (#1 = .39; #2 = .54; #3 = .74; #4 = .67; #5 =
.58) and averaged. The average of the coefficients is
.58, a fair correlation. For, even as Diederich reports
in his own research, for example, a correlation such as
.67 is "far from satisfactory, but it is typical. . . . I
have rarely been able to boost the average correlation
between pairs of readers above .50, and other examiners
tell me that this is about whay they get" (1974, p. 33).

Figure 5.45. Editing a technical publication for artistry (cont'd).

Evaluation   page 18

(Times 8/12)

Table 1
Writing Apprehension Results (Daly-Miller)

(Ital)

	M		t
	Pre	Post	
Control[a]	72.5	76.2	-2.21*
Experimental[b]	68.7	72.3	-2.16*

(ital)
(ital)

$^a\underline{n}$ = 52. $^b\underline{n}$ = 103.
*$\underline{p}$<.05.

Table 2
Writing Apprehension Sub-scale Results

(ital)

	M		t
	Pre	Post	
Control[a]	32.3	31.9	0.86
Experimental[b]	32.6	31.7	2.68*

(ital)
(ital)

$^a\underline{n}$ = 52. $^b\underline{n}$ = 103.
*$\underline{p}$<.01.

Table 3
Improvement in Writing Quality

(ital)

	M		t
	Pre	Post	
Control[a]	78.3	78.7	-0.42*
Experimental[b]	75.3	77.4	-3.01*

(ital)
(ital)

$^a\underline{n}$ = 52. $^b\underline{n}$ = 103.
*$\underline{p}$<.01.

Figure 5.45.   Editing a technical publication for artistry (cont'd).

Results and Discussion

Writing Apprehension

Table 1 presents the results of the 2 two-tailed *t*-tests for the changes in response to the Daly-Miller Writing Apprehension Test (1975).

Table 1
Writing Apprehension Results (Daly-Miller)

| | M | | *t* |
	Pre	Post	
Control[a]	72.5	76.2	-2.21*
Experimental[b]	68.7	72.3	-2.16*

[a]$n = 52.$ [b]$n = 103.$
*$p < .05$.

Curiously, students in both the control and the experimental groups showed significant increases in apprehension across the semester ($t = -2.21, t = -2.16, p < .05$). The small but significant increases in apprehension were clearly not expected, and, perhaps equally important, did not distinguish between the control and experimental group.

To test for the possibility that the Daly-Miller, as a whole, was not sensitive enough to pick up differences in students' attitudes toward evaluation of their writing, a subscale of ten items was created from that test. These ten items—1, 2, 4, 6, 12, 18, 22, and 25—all probe students' attitudes about having others read their writing and about having their essays evaluated. Table 2 presents the results.

Table 2
Writing Apprehension Sub-scale Results

| | M | | *t* |
	Pre	Post	
Control[a]	32.3	31.9	0.86
Experimental[b]	32.6	31.7	2.68*

[a]$n = 52.$ [b]$n = 103.$
*$p < .01$.

Figure 5.45. Editing a technical publication for artistry (cont'd).

<u>58</u>

Although the control group did not show significant decreases on these ten items ($t = 0.86$, $p > .05$), the experimental group improved significantly ($t = 2.68$, $p < .01$). Student writers in the experimental group responded positively to the one-to-one conferences in which they discussed their writing and suggestions for guided ation process in the experimental group when their essays were rated the same by two outside readers. The rater agreement and guidelines for revision seemed to put these students more at ease about writing for other readers and submitting essays for evaluation.

Two interesting questions emerge from the subscale results, where students' overall apprehension increased but their apprehension about evaluation decreased: Is writing apprehension as influential and important an entity as the Daly-Miller assumes it is? And how sensitive is this test as an indicator of apprehension?

Writing Quality

Two different procedures were used for determining writing quality in the two groups. Control group essays were graded in the traditional manner (A, B, C, etc.); experimental group essays were evaluated holistically on a 0-100 scale. This difference coupled with the fact that different topics for the expressive, referential, and persuasive essays were used to measure pre- and post-course writing quality make it impossible to compare the two groups directly. Nevertheless, improvement over the semester can be at least estimated by comparing grades on an early and later paper for the control group and by comparing holistic scores of an early and a later paper for the experimental group.

In the first case, the results seemed valid in light of the fact that the instructors' grades were purely dependent on the perceived quality of the writing (i.e., not influenced by pedagogical considerations) and the writing tasks chosen from the beginning and end of the semester made roughly the same demands on the student writers. In the second case, the results seemed valid in light of the fact that the raters evaluated the pre- and post-essays on the same scale and the writing tasks were equivalent.

Table 3 shows an estimate of the improvement in writing quality over the semester based on the comparison of early and later papers described above. Given the validity of the results, the data suggest that both groups improved significantly in writing quality.

Table 3
Improvement in Writing Quality

	M		t
	Pre	Post	
Control[a]	78.3	78.7	-0.42*
Experimental[b]	75.3	77.4	-3.01*

[a]$n = 52$. [b]$n = 103$.
*$p < .01$.

Figure 5.45. Editing a technical publication for artistry (cont'd).

59

The control group showed some increase in writing quality from the expressive essay to the persuasive essay $(t = -0.42, p < .01)$. However, the experimental group made extraordinary progress from essay 1 to essay 5 $(t = -3.01, p < .01)$. Again, though the grades of students whose work had been evaluated traditionally steadily increased, their progress was not commensurate with the increase in quality of those students whose writing had been evaluated both by summative and formative techniques. The guided revision and one-to-one conferencing seemed to increase the writing abilities of students significantly .

To measure the reliability of raters of the experimental group's essays, a Spearman's Rho (i.e., a type of correlation between rank order data) was used. The correlation coefficients for each of the five essays were determined (#1 = .39; #2 = .54; #3 = .74; #4 = .67; #5 = .58) and averaged. The average of the coefficients is .58, a fair correlation. For, even as Diederich reports in his own research, for example, a correlation such as .67 is "far from satisfactory, but it is typical. . . . I have rarely been able to boost the average correlation between pairs of readers above .50, and other examiners tell me that this is about whay they get" (1974, p. 33).

Figure 5.45. Editing a technical publication for artistry (cont'd).

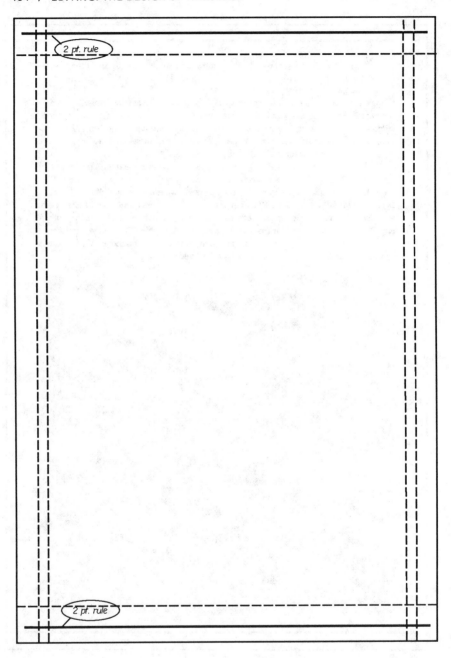

Figure 5.45. Editing a technical publication for artistry (cont'd).

	Printing	Paper	Folding/Binding	Typography	Illustrations	Page Design
Aim	lithographic for high quality	medium weight for durability	saddle wire or perfect for quasi-durability	sans serif for technical info	simple tables	1 column for clear sequencing of info
Audience	lithographic for prestige		traditional saddle wire or perfect	traditional 10 pt. serif, justified text	simple tables	traditional 1 column
Verbal Information		smooth, un-coated for readability		traditional 10 pt. serif, aligned left, ragged right	top/bottom rules to emphasize equivalency	1 column for unity of info
Visual Information		smooth un-coated for crisp image		subordinate 8 pt. serif for tables, justified text	unboxed tables to integrate with text	1 column for unity of info

Figure 5.46.   Delivery matrix for the technical publication.

2. *What is the basic point size of type? What retinal variations of size occur? What is their significance?*
The basic type size is 10 point, with no variations of size occurring. This emphasizes the equivalent importance of various blocks of information, as is appropriate to a traditional objective report of research findings.
3. *What is the basic style of type? What retinal variations of style occur? What is their significance?*
The basic style of type is plain, positive image, achromatic, upper/lower case. Bold and italic styles also occur. The bold headings, with their dramatic change of value, dominate the blocks of information. The italic type, with its shift of orientation, is sufficiently distinctive from the plain type of the information blocks to serve as subheadings.
4. *What is the basic horizontal and vertical spacing? What retinal variations of spacing occur? What is their significance?*
Line length is a conventional 5 inches (30 picas), justified left and right, with 2 points of leading. Though left aligned and ragged right type offers superior readability, the uniformity of the justified columns effectively boxes the tables on the page. The heading is centered, with the subheadings aligned on the left. The variation in spacing yields three different textures, with the heading, the subheadings, and the verbal discussion obviously distinctive.

Illustrations: Tables

1. *What are the typographical characteristics of each table? What retinal variations of design, size, style, and spacing occur? What is their significance?*
In the tables, the type is a plain serif, 8 point with 4 points of leading, a line length of 4 inches (24 picas), justified left and right. Italics occur to identify statistical symbols. Differences in size and texture allow the type used in the verbal discussion to dominate that used in the tables, emphasizing the importance of the verbal discussion.
2. *What are the illustrative characteristics of each table? What retinal variations of the illustrative characteristics occur? What is the significance of the retinal variations?*
No illustrative characteristics occur. The exclusively typographical design of the tables allows the association of the tables with the verbal discussion.

Illustrations: Figures

1. *What are the illustrative characteristics of each figure? What retinal variations of the illustrative characteristics occur? What is the significance of the retinal variations?*
Not applicable.

2. *What are the typographical characteristics of each figure? What retinal varia-tions of design, size, style, and spacing occur? What is their significance?*
   Not applicable
3. *Do the illustrative and typographical characteristics of each figure communi-cate or reinforce a single and unified meaning?*
   Not applicable
4. *Does each figure encourage viewing as opposed to reading? How is this achieved?*
   Not applicable

Page Design

1. *What is the basic page grid? What retinal variations of this page grid occur? What is the significance of the retinal variations?*
   The basic page grid is a single 5-inch column, with left and right margins of 1.5 inches. This directs the reader's eye sequentially through each page. The only variation comes with the insertion of the tables and their additional white space on the left and right. The verbal discussion's 5-inch column dominates the 4-inch columns of the tables, emphasizing the superior impor-tance of the verbal discussion.
2. *Which pages of the publication deserve the reader's initial attention? the reader's subsequent attention? Why? Do these pages solicit this attention? How?*
   The information blocks have been designed to allow association of the in-formation, and the verbal equivalence of the pages is visually reinforced with top and bottom 2-point rules. The page beginning this section of the research report, however, with its two tables and additional surrounding white space, does look especially inviting or easy to read. This is desirable.
3. *Which illustrations on each page deserve the reader's initial attention? the reader's subsequent attention? Why? Do these illustrations solicit this atten-tion? How?*
   All illustrations have been identically designed because no special or initial attention to a given illustration is necessary or appropriate. Each of the tables is important and their similarity of design allows association of their informa-tion.
4. *Which blocks of typography on each page deserve the reader's initial atten-tion? the reader's subsequent attention? Why? Do these blocks of typography solicit this attention? How?*
   All information blocks have been given identical typographical designs to emphasize their equivalence. This is reinforced with subheadings that equal the type size of their pertinent discussions, but differ in orientation, thereby exploiting selectivity instead of proportion.

Production

1. *Does the printing process harmonize with the typography, illustrations, and page design?*
To publish sufficient copies of a quality appropriate to a professional journal and satisfactory to its audience, a lithographic printing process is likely: this process has no deleterious effect on the typography, illustrations, or page design. The specifications prove neither elaborate nor exotic.
2. *Does the paper harmonize with the typography, illustrations, and page design?*
This technical publication is verbally oriented, with single columns of text interrupted only by tables of verbal information; it is likely to receive only periodic reading or reviewing. A smooth, uncoated paper of medium weight and thickness is therefore appropriate.
3. *Does the folding/binding process harmonize with the typography, illustrations, and page design?*
Typical of professional journals is either a saddle-wire or perfect binding. A saddle-wire binding might allow illustrations to bleed to or across the inner margins of the verso and recto pages, whereas a perfect binding proscribes this page design. This verbally oriented technical publication, however, has no illustrations that justify bleeding. Either folding/binding process is also satisfactory for durability requirements: it is likely that personal copies of the journal receive a single reading and periodic review. And though library copies of the journal receive multiple readings, the issues of a designated period are routinely compiled with a sewn binding.

A News Publication

This sample is a brief article from the newsletter of a professional association (see Figure 5.47). The accompanying matrix (see Figure 5.48) displays the editor's delivery choices.

Typography

1. *What are the characteristics of the basic type design? What retinal variations of design occur? What is their significance?*
The basic type design is serif, with average x-height, wide counters, average ascenders and descenders, obvious variation between thicks and thins, and clear vertical stress. This is a traditional type design, suitable for this verbally oriented document: the wide enclosed spaces of the letters give the words a look of simplicity and accessibility. No variation of this design occurs, thereby keeping the information blocks associated.

set head 24/26
Century Schoolbook
(fl) (ital)

set text 10/12
Century Schoolbook
(ital)

(ital)

Texas Liberal Review Converts to Desktop Publishing

Continuity will mark upcoming issues of the **Texas Liberal Review** even as we move away from old-fashioned typesetting to desktop publishing in producing the journal. If all goes as planned, the Spring 1988 issue will match the style, format, and quality of earlier issues while being produced by radically different means. Instead of having the Texas State Printing Center typeset articles for the **Texas Liberal Review**, we plan to capture authors' keystrokes whenever possible. With funds from both the Texas Association for Liberal Critical Inquiry and Texas State University, we have purchased equipment that should allow us to produce galley proofs in the editorial office without having to pay for typesetting services. The savings should be substantial, allowing TALCI to recoup its investment in less than a year.

For those interested in a detailed description of the equipment ("robot talk" as one of our colleagues calls it), we have a Compaq Deskpro 286 computer (with a 30 megabyte hard drive and a 5-1/4 inch floppy disk drive), an Apple LaserWriter Plus printer, a full-page portrait monitor, and a Microsoft serial mouse. The software for our system runs on the MS-DOS Version 3 operating system. We will be using WordPositor word processing software in conjunction with the PositivePublisher page layout software.Those authors who create electronic manuscripts processed in WordPositor (MS-DOS, 5-1/4 inch floppy) will produce material most compatible with our system; however, we should be able to accomodate any document converted to a DOS/ASCII file.

More information will be supplied later as we learn about our abilities (and inabilities) to convert files from various word processing programs, from different operating systems, and from several sizes of microcomputer disks. For now, all authors—those who work at typewriters and those who work at word processors—should continue to submit two paper ("hard") copies of manuscripts for evalution by readers. Once an article is accepted, we will request a disk from the author if the work was prepared on a word processor.

Figure 5.47. Editing a news publication for artistry.

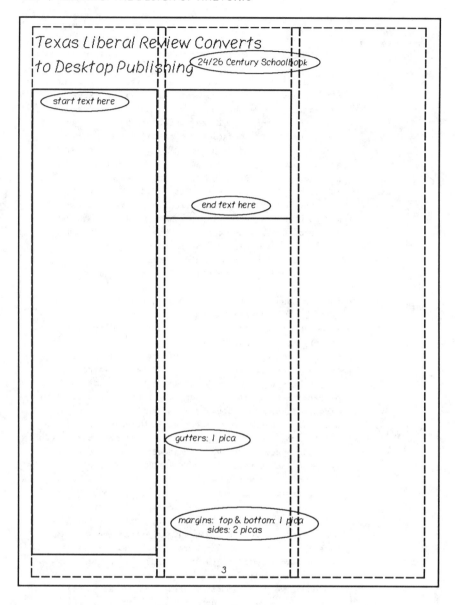

Texas Liberal Review Converts to Desktop Publishing
24/26 Century Schoolbook

start text here

end text here

gutters: 1 pica

margins: top & bottom: 1 pica
sides: 2 picas

3

Figure 5.47.   Editing a news publication for artistry (cont'd).

Texas Liberal Review Converts to Desktop Publishing

Continuity will mark upcoming issues of the *Texas Liberal Review* even as we move away from old-fashioned typesetting to desktop publishing in producing the journal. If all goes as planned, the Spring 1988 issue will match the style, format, and quality of earlier issues while being produced by radically different means. Instead of having the Texas State Printing Center typeset articles for the *Texas Liberal Review,* we plan to capture authors' keystrokes whenever possible. With funds from both the Texas Association for Liberal Critical Inquiry and Texas State University, we have purchased equipment that should allow us to produce galley proofs in the editorial office without having to pay for typesetting services. The savings should be substantial, allowing TALCI to recoup its investment in less than a year.

For those interested in a detailed description of the equipment ("robot talk" as one of our colleagues calls it), we have a Compaq Deskpro 286 computer (with a 30 megabyte hard drive and a 5-1/4 inch floppy disk drive), an Apple LaserWriter Plus printer, a full-page portrait monitor, and a Microsoft serial mouse. The software for our system runs on the MS-DOS Version 3 operating system. We will be using WordPositor word processing software in conjunction with the Positive-Publisher page layout software. Those authors who create electronic manuscripts processed in WordPositor (MS-DOS, 5-1/4 inch floppy) will produce material most compatible with our system; however, we should be able to accomodate any document converted to a DOS/ASCII file.

More information will be supplied later as we learn about our abilities (and inabilities) to convert files from various word processing programs, from different operating systems, and from several sizes of microcomputer disks. For now, all authors—those who work at typewriters and those who work at word processors—should continue to submit two paper ("hard") copies of manuscripts for evaluation by readers. Once an article is accepted, we will request a disk from the author if the work was prepared on a word processor.

3

Figure 5.47. Editing a news publication for artistry (cont'd).

	Printing	Paper	Folding/Binding	Typography	Illustrations	Page Design
Aim	lithographic for high quality	light weight for single reading	zero binding for single reading	traditional 10 pt. serif		multicolumn for flexible emphasis
Audience	lithographic for prestige	medium weight for prestige	traditional zero binding satisfies expectations	traditional 10 pt. serif, justified text		traditional 3 columns
Verbal Information		smooth, un-coated for readability		traditional 10 pt. serif, aligned left, ragged right		3 columns for readability
Visual Information						

Figure 5.48. Delivery matrix for the news publication.

2. *What is the basic point size of type? What retinal variations of size occur? What is their significance?*

   The basic type size is 10 point, with a heading of 24 point. The dominance of the heading is thus obvious.

3. *What is the basic style of type? What retinal variations of style occur? What is their significance?*

   The basic style of type is plain, positive image, achromatic, upper/lower case. Italic style is used to identify the title of the journal, once in the heading and twice in the opening paragraph. The shift of orientation is conventional, here distinguishing the journal from information regarding its publication.

4. *What is the basic horizontal and vertical spacing? What retinal variations of spacing occur? What is their significance?*

   Line length is 2.5 inches (15 picas), justified left and right, with 2 points of leading. The short line is typical of a news publication and gives the impression of quick passage through the verbal information as the reader's eye moves across and down the narrow columns. The heading is aligned left, with a ragged right: the second shorter line of the heading serves to pull the reader's eye to the left margin again, to the following line and the opening paragraph. The variation of texture reinforces the variation of size.

Illustrations: Tables

1. *What are the typographical characteristics of each table? What retinal variations of design, size, style, and spacing occur? What is their significance?*

   Not applicable

2. *What are the illustrative characteristics of each table? What retinal variations of the illustrative characteristics occur? What is the significance of the retinal variations?*

   Not applicable

Illustrations: Figures

1. *What are the illustrative characteristics of each figure? What retinal variations of the illustrative characteristics occur? What is the significance of the retinal variations?*

   Not applicable

2. *What are the typographical characteristics of each figure? What retinal variations of design, size, style, and spacing occur? What is their significance?*

   Not applicable

3. *Do the illustrative and typographical characteristics of each figure communicate or reinforce a single and unified meaning?*

   Not applicable

4. Does each figure encourage viewing as opposed to reading? How is this achieved?

Not applicable

Page Design

1. What is the basic page grid? What retinal variations of this page grid occur? What is the significance of the retinal variations?

The basic page grid is three columns of 15 picas, with left and right margins of 2 picas, top and bottom margins of 1 pica, and gutters of 1 pica. The only variation of this grid is the two column heading, appropriately dominating the single column paragraphs.

2. Which pages of the publication deserve the reader's initial attention; the reader's subsequent attention? Why? Do these pages solicit this attention? How?

The pages of this publication solicit attention according to the size and position of the headings of the individual news pieces. This article, occurring on the inside margin of the inside recto page, has a 24-point heading that dominates only two columns of the page: on the cover, a heading of three columns and at least 24 points or two columns and at least 30 points is necessary to signal superiority to this inside heading.

3. Which illustrations on each page deserve the reader's initial attention? the reader's subsequent attention? Why? Do these illustrations solicit this attention? How?

Not applicable

4. Which blocks of typography on each page deserve the reader's initial attention? the reader's subsequent attention? Why? Do these blocks of typography solicit this attention? How?

All information blocks have been given identical typographical designs to emphasize their associated subject. The differing sizes of the headings signal the priority of the individual news pieces.

Production

1. Does the printing process harmonize with the typography, illustrations, and page design?

To publish sufficient copies of a quality appropriate to the newsletter of a professional association, a lithographic printing process is likely. This process easily satisfies the simple and conventional specifications regarding typography and page design.

2. Does the paper harmonize with the typography, illustrations, and page design?

This news publication is verbally oriented and likely to receive a single reading. A relatively smooth, uncoated paper of light weight and little thickness is sufficient, though a medium weight might prove necessary to establish prestige and credibility.

3. *Does the folding/binding process harmonize with the typography, illustrations, and page design?*
A zero binding is necessary to the narrow inner margins of the page design. It would also allow illustrations (e.g., pictures of meetings of the association, maps of meeting sites) to bleed to or across the inner margins, as necessary.

A Promotional Publication

This sample of a promotional publication is distributed by the Department of English, Texas A&M University (see Figure 5.49). The accompanying matrix (see Figure 5.50) displays the editor's choices regarding delivery.

Typography

1. *What are the characteristics of the basic type design? What retinal variations of design occur? What is their significance?*
The basic type design is serif, with average x-height, wide counters, average ascenders and descenders, obvious variation between thicks and thins, and clear vertical stress. This conventional type design is suitable for the verbal passages of this visually oriented document: the wide enclosed spaces of the letters give the impression that this information is easy to read, easy to understand. Variations of type design do occur: a sans serif imitative of the type design available on word processors and a sans serif imitative of handwriting. The variations of design serve to distinguish the different blocks of information.
2. *What is the basic point size of type? What retinal variations of size occur? What is their significance?*
The basic type size is 12 point, with headings of 18, 30, and 48 points, signalling levels of superiority.
3. *What is the basic style of type? What retinal variations of style occur? What is their significance?*
The basic style of type is plain, positive image, achromatic, upper/lower case. Bold is the style of all headings, the words *The Writing Specialization*, and course designations. Course titles have been italicized. The variations of style allow the information to be accessed several ways. The bold headings and course designations compose a capsulized version of the promotional publication, identifying the program and its core courses: the bolding allows the reader to focus on this information, and ignore the remainder. The italic

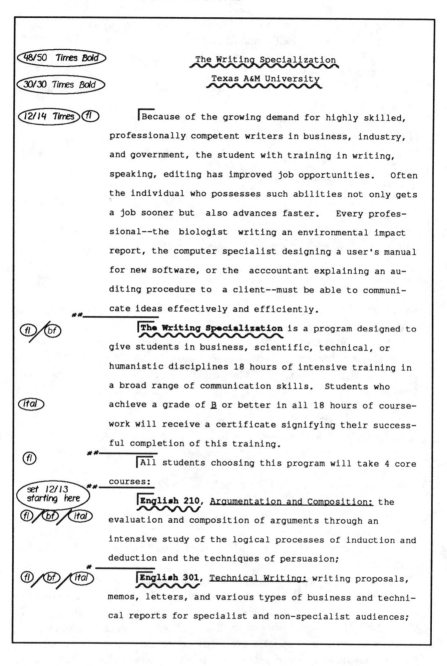

The Writing Specialization
Texas A&M University

48/50 Times Bold

30/30 Times Bold

12/14 Times (fl)

Because of the growing demand for highly skilled, professionally competent writers in business, industry, and government, the student with training in writing, speaking, editing has improved job opportunities. Often the individual who possesses such abilities not only gets a job sooner but also advances faster. Every professional--the biologist writing an environmental impact report, the computer specialist designing a user's manual for new software, or the acccountant explaining an auditing procedure to a client--must be able to communicate ideas effectively and efficiently.

(fl) (bf)

The Writing Specialization is a program designed to give students in business, scientific, technical, or humanistic disciplines 18 hours of intensive training in a broad range of communication skills. Students who

(ital)

achieve a grade of B or better in all 18 hours of coursework will receive a certificate signifying their successful completion of this training.

(fl)

All students choosing this program will take 4 core courses:

set 12/13 starting here
(fl) (bf) (ital)

English 210, _Argumentation and Composition:_ the evaluation and composition of arguments through an intensive study of the logical processes of induction and deduction and the techniques of persuasion;

(fl) (bf) (ital)

English 301, _Technical Writing:_ writing proposals, memos, letters, and various types of business and technical reports for specialist and non-specialist audiences;

Figure 5.49. Editing a promotional publication for artistry.

(fl) (bf) (ital)

English 320, <u>Technical Editing:</u> the study and practice of the rhetorical skills required of professional editors, from copyediting and proofreading to document design and desktop publishing;

(fl) (bf) (ital)

Speech Communication 404, <u>Technical and Professional Speaking:</u> composing and delivering oral presentations of technical material using various media.

(resume 12/14) (fl)

In addition, students will select 6 hours of supporting courses, usually connected with their major. Students, in consultation with the Writing Specialization Coordinator in the Department of English, can thereby create their own program of special emphasis.

(fl) (bf)

To register for the **The Writing Specialization** or to receive more information about it, contact Sam Dragga (409-845-8304), 201D Blocker Building, Department of English, Texas A&M University, College Station, TX 77843.

(18/18 Times Bold)

The Writing Specialization

(and 3 figures (see attached page design))

Figure 5.49. Editing a promotional publication for artistry (cont'd).

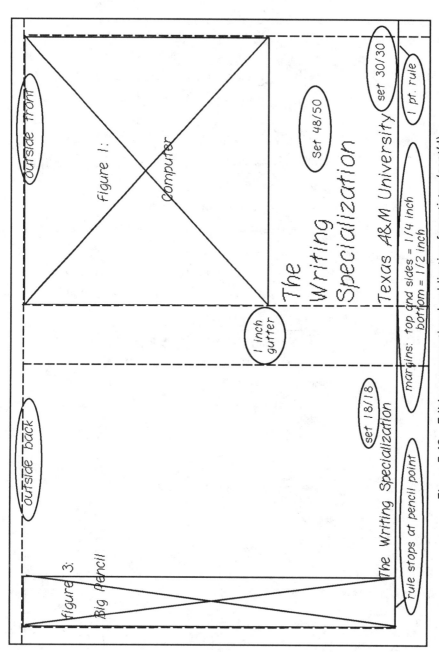

Figure 5.49. Editing a promotional publication for artistry (cont'd).

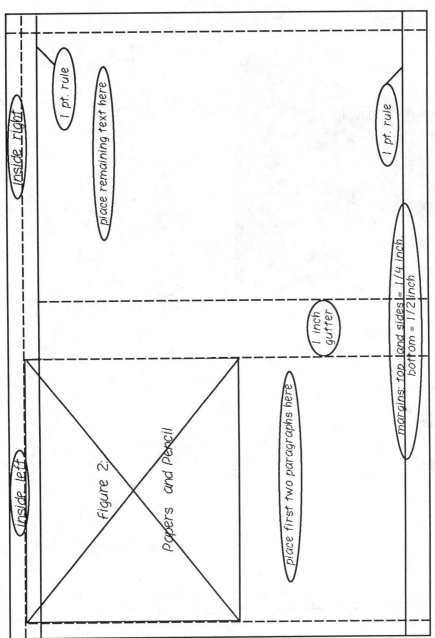

Figure 5.49. Editing a promotional publication for artistry (cont'd).

Figure 5.49. Editing a promotional publication for artistry (cont'd).

Because of the growing demand for highly skilled, professionally competent writers in business, industry, and government, the student with training in writing, speaking, and editing has improved job opportunities. Often the individual who possesses such abilities not only gets a job sooner but also advances faster. Every professional—the biologist writing an environmental impact report, the computer specialist designing a user's manual for new software, or the accountant explaining an auditing procedure to a client—must be able to communicate ideas effectively and efficiently.

The Writing Specialization is a program designed to give students in business, scientific, technical, or humanistic disciplines 18 hours of intensive training in a broad range of communication skills. Students who achieve a grade of *B* or better in all 18 hours of coursework will receive a certificate signifying their successful completion of this training.

All students choosing this program will take 4 core courses:

English 210, *Argumentation and Composition*: the evaluation and composition of arguments through an intensive study of the logical processes of induction and deduction and the techniques of persuasion;

English 301, *Technical Writing*: writing proposals, memos, letters, and various types of business and technical reports for specialist and non-specialist audiences;

English 320, *Technical Editing*: the study and practice of the rhetorical skills required of professional editors, from copy-editing and proofreading to document design and desktop publishing;

Speech Communication 404, *Technical and Professional Speaking*: composing and delivering oral presentations of technical material using various media.

In addition, students will select 6 hours of supporting courses, usually connected with their major. Students, in consultation with the Writing Specialization Coordinator in the Department of English, can thereby create their own program of special emphasis.

To register for the **The Writing Specialization** or to receive more information about it, contact Sam Dragga (409-845-8304), 201D Blocker Building, Department of English, Texas A&M University, College Station, TX 77843.

Figure 5.49. Editing a promotional publication for artistry (cont'd).

	Printing	Paper	Folding/ Binding	Typography	Illustrations	Page Design
Aim	lithographic for high quality	glossy coated for prestige	bifold for simplicity	traditional serif	creative, attractive drawings	clean, simple
Audience	lithographic for prestige	glossy coated for prestige	bifold for quick access		drawings obviously associated with writing	clean, simple
Verbal Information		dull coated for readability		traditional 10 pt serif, aligned left, ragged right	reinforce text, rules guide eye to text	1 column for unity of info
Visual Information		glossy coated for crisp image	bifold to allow big drawings	imitative sans serif	reinforce, dominate text	1 column for big, attractive drawings

Figure 5.50. Delivery matrix for the promotional publication.

type of the course titles, with its shift of orientation, is also sufficiently distinctive from the plain type of the course descriptions to allow selective perception of either.

4. *What is the basic horizontal and vertical spacing? What retinal variations of spacing occur? What is their significance?*
Type is aligned left with a ragged right. The leading of the paragraphs is two points, switching to one point for the course descriptions. The resulting difference of texture encourages readers to perceive the four courses as a core as well as to distinguish between requirements of the Writing Specialization and requirements of individual courses within the program.

Illustrations: Tables

1. *What are the typographical characteristics of each table? What retinal variations of design, size, style, and spacing occur? What is their significance?*
Not applicable

2. *What are the illustrative characteristics of each table? What retinal variations of the illustrative characteristics occur? What is the significance of the retinal variations?*
Not applicable

Illustrations: Figures

1. *What are the illustrative characteristics of each figure? What retinal variations of the illustrative characteristics occur? What is the significance of the retinal variations?*
Three figures occur, all drawings: a microcomputer, a big pencil, and a pencil and paper. Though none of the pictures is realistic, the imitative type designs do serve to heighten this impression. The drawing of the microcomputer uses identical textures to unify the image and different values to separate the components and give them dimension, replicating the similarity of the materials used in the composition of microcomputers. The drawing of the big pencil, as well as the pencil and paper, uses a variety of both values and textures to picture the different materials that compose a pencil: graphite, wood, metal, and rubber. In addition, on the bottom of the outside pages and on the top and bottom of the inside pages, 2-point rules have been incorporated. The rule on the outside page is positioned as though drawn by the big pencil, and establishes a horizon for the drawings. On the inside pages, the rules enclose the verbal information, but fail to restrain the drawing: the simple and fairly unimaginative drawing of the pencil and paper breaks through the top line and, as a consequence, seems relatively dynamic or aggressive.

2. *What are the typographical characteristics of each figure? What retinal varia-tions of design, size, style, and spacing occur? What is their significance?*
The microcomputer drawing uses a 6-point, sans serif type design to imitate the type available on word processors. Similarly, the pencil and paper draw-ing uses a 6-point, sans serif type design to imitate handwriting.

3. *Do the illustrative and typographical characteristics of each figure com-municate or reinforce a single and unified meaning?*
The microcomputer drawing and the sans serif type design give a unified impression of a writer composing on a word processor. Similarly, the pencil and paper drawing and its sans serif type design imitate a handwritten com-position.

4. *Does each figure encourage viewing as opposed to reading? How is this achieved?*
Each of the figures encourages viewing as opposed to reading. In the figures with type, the typographical material is brief and the type size small enough to discourage reading. It seems evident that the type is used only to heighten the reader's perception of the drawings as relatively realistic and thus serious.

Page Design

1. *What is the basic page grid? What retinal variations of this page grid occur? What is the significance of the retinal variations?*
The basic page grid is two columns of 4.5 inches each (27 picas), with left and right and top and bottom margins of 1/2 inch (3 picas), and a gutter of 1 inch (6 picas). No variation of this design occurs.

2. *Which pages of the publication deserve the reader's initial attention? the reader's subsequent attention? Why? Do these pages solicit this attention? How?*
The outside front page of the publication solicits the reader's initial atten-tion, with its drawing and its bold 48-point and 30-point heading. The words of the heading have been positioned as a virtual staircase leading the reader's eye to the lower right corner of the page and on to the inside of the promo-tional publication. If the reader, however, flips the publication over, the big pencil drawing on the outside back page stands as a vertical barrier, keeping the reader from moving to the inside pages; instead the 2-point rule, appear-ing to come from the pencil, pulls the reader's eye back to the outside front page and on to the inside pages. Here, the reader's eye goes immediately to the visual on the inside left page, then to the verbal information on the inside left and right pages.

3. *Which illustrations on each page deserve the reader's initial attention? the reader's subsequent attention? Why? Do these illustrations solicit this atten-tion? How?*
With a single illustration on each page of the publication, there is no compe-

tition among the drawings for the reader's attention. Given the complexity of the microcomputer drawing, it seems likely that readers will give this initial and special attention. It is also likely that the unimpressive inside drawing of the pencil and paper will receive a cursory viewing: this is desirable because it is the verbal information on the inside pages that deserves the reader's attention. The chief attraction of the drawing of the big pencil is its size.

4. *Which blocks of typography on each page deserve the reader's initial attention? the reader's subsequent attention? Why? Do these blocks of typography solicit this attention? How?*
On the outside front page, the 48-point heading solicits initial attention and the 30-point heading subsequent attention. On the inside pages, it is likely that the course descriptions to the right of the drawing receive the reader's immediate attention: the bold course designations, italicized course titles, and variations of texture all prove especially attractive to the eye. Following this, the reader is likely to move down the inside right page and across to the inside left, quite possibly saving the first paragraph for last.

Production

1. *Does the printing process harmonize with the typography, illustrations, and page design?*
Given the limited aim and audience of this publication, a xerographic printing process is satisfactory, though a lithographic process brings the prestige of superior quality. Either process might easily satisfy the specifications regarding typography, illustrations, and page design. This promotional publication, however, does have a complex mix of verbal and visual material, and the xerographic process does require the writer's or editor's preparation of a camera copy.

2. *Does the paper harmonize with the typography, illustrations, and page design?*
A coated paper of medium weight with a dull finish gives this promotional publication the prestige and durability essential to its persuasive aim and to its audience of college students. A coated paper also allows a crisp reproduction of the drawings, and a dull finish improves readability of the typographical material.

3. *Does the folding/binding process harmonize with the typography, illustrations, and page design?*
A bifold publication accords with the quantity and quality of the verbal and visual information, offering a judicious balance of words, pictures, and white space. It also leaves the information easily accessed, as is necessary to its aim and audience.

REFERENCES

1. D. J. Ochs, Cicero's Rhetorical Theory, in *A Synoptic History of Classical Rhetoric*. J. J. Murphy (ed.), Hermagoras Press, Davis, California, pp. 90–150, 1983.
2. R. J. Connors, *Actio*: A Rhetoric of Manuscripts, *Rhetoric Review, 2*, 1983, pp. 64–73.
3. J. Bertin, *Semiology of Graphics*, W. J. Berg (trans.), University of Wisconsin Press, Madison, 1983.
4. G. M. Murch, Using Color Effectively: Designing to Human Specifications, *Technical Communication, 32*, 1985, pp. 14–20.
5. R. W. Burnham, R. M. Hanes, and C. J. Bartelson, *Color: A Guide to Basic Facts and Concepts*, Wiley, New York, 1963.
6. C. Burt, *A Psychological Study of Typography*, Cambridge University Press, Cambridge, 1959.
7. B. Zachrisson, *Studies in Legibility of Printed Text*, Almqvist and Wiskell, Stockholm, 1965.
8. M. A. Tinker, *Legibility of Print*, Iowa State University Press, Ames, 1963.
9. J. Craig, *Designing with Type*, rev. edition, Watson-Guptill, New York, 1980.
10. E. Goldsmith, *Research into Illustration*, Cambridge University Press, Cambridge, 1984.
11. H. F. Brandt, *The Psychology of Seeing*, Philosophical Library, New York, 1945.

Epilogue:
Integrating the Canons

We have considered the rhetorical canons of invention, arrangement, style, and delivery and the corresponding editorial objectives of accuracy, clarity, propriety, and artistry. This isolation of the canons, however, disguises the complexity and creativity of the editor's job. Editing is a fluid and recursive process requiring the integration of the canons. The editor's decisions on accuracy, for example, influence his or her ideas on clarity, propriety, and artistry, and vice versa. Editing is thus never a static series of discrete analyses: it is a dynamic array of simultaneous and interactive evaluations (see Figure E.1).

In addition, editing always occurs within the limits of time and money, usually sacrificing the desirable for the feasible. The editor is thus always adjusting and compromising, always determining how thorough a job of editing is necessary, how close to the ideal it is possible to bring a given discourse. For example, the editor might ignore minor typographical errors because serious grammatical errors occupy his or her limited time. Similarly, though a color diagram might be especially fitting, a satisfactory artist might be unavailable or the cost of color might be prohibitive.

It is thus impossible to identify a single process of editing that is always satisfactory. If the text is brief or time is short, a single reading is often sufficient. Just as often, however, a second or third reading is necessary, especially if the subject is complex, if the audience is mixed, or if the discourse has subordinate aims. Occasionally it is possible to dedicate each reading to a specific level of editing (e.g., wording or mechanics), though typically the editor tries to address all issues without delay. Similarly, the process of editing differs according to the editor's responsibilities to the writer (e.g., assessing only writing style or also reviewing the accuracy and clarity of the discourse) as well as the editor's responsibilities to compositors and artists (e.g., supplying only the camera copy of visuals or also choosing the type and determining the page design). Explicit rhetorical analysis using the editor's inventories for invention, arrangement, style, and delivery is thus especially important to the beginning editor. The experienced editor, however, consciously or unconsciously comes to internalize this series of questions, achieving the holistic perspective necessary to the integration of the canons and the judicious mediation of the writer-reader relationship.

Invention Inventory

Communicative Aim
1. What does the writer perceive to be the communicative aim? Is it Expressive? Referential? Persuasive? Literary?
2. Is the communicative aim clearly identified or explained in the text?
3. Are there subordinate aims in the text? If so, what are they? Are they appropriate for this text?

Audience
1. Who does the writer perceive to be the primary audience for this text?
2. Who does the writer perceive to be the secondary audience for this text?
3. Has the writer appropriately analyzed the primary and secondary audiences according to
   - Level of education?
   - Professional experience?
   - Familiarity with subject?
   - Expectations?
   - Enthusiasm?
   - Urgency?
   - Environment
4. Has the writer invoked the appropriate audience?

Information Gathering
1. Has the writer gathered appropriate information?
2. Has the writer gathered sufficient information?
3. Are the information sources reliable?
4. Is the information plausible?
5. Is the information consistent?

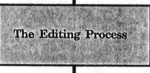

Arrangement Inventory

Verbal-Visual Orientation
1. What does the writer perceive to be the verbal-visual orientation of the text?
2. Is this orientation appropriate?

Principles and Diagrams of Organization
1. What is the organization of the discourse? Spatial? Chronological? Hierarchical? Categorical?
2. How might the text be diagrammed? Line? Circle? Pyramid? Funnel? String of Beads? Braid?
3. Is this organization appropriate to the aim of the discourse? Does it serve to clarify the information?
4. Is the organization appropriate to the audience of the discourse? Does it help readers to assimilate the information?

Coherence and Cohesion
1. Does the writer establish a chain of given/new information? Is this chain achieved through repetition, substitution, or equivalence?
2. Does the writer use sufficient and appropriate transitions?
3. Does the writer use parallel wording and phrasing as necessary?
4. Does the writer use sufficient and appropriate headings? Are the coordinate and subordinate headings clearly and logically arranged?
5. Does the size, value, and position of headings clearly indicate their degree of importance?

Figure E.1. Integrating the canons.

Style Inventory

Verbal Propriety
1. What are the verbal style characteristics of discourse medium and participation, province, status, and modality?
2. What are the verbal style characteristics of individuality, dialect, time, and singularity?
3. Do the verbal style characteristics of discourse medium and participation, province, status, and modality dominate the verbal style characteristics of individuality, dialect, time, and singularity?
4. Is the verbal style consistent across the lexical, grammatical, and mechanical levels of the text?

Visual Propriety
1. What are the visual style characteristics of discourse medium and participation, province, status, and modality?
2. What are the visual style characteristics of individuality, dialect, time, and singularity?
3. Do the visual style characteristics of discourse medium and participation, province, status, and modality dominate the visual style characteristics of individuality, dialect, time, and singularity?
4. Is the visual style consistent across the lexical, grammatical, and mechanical levels of the discourse?

Delivery Inventory

Typography
1. What are the characteristics of the basic type design (i.e., serif/sans serif, x-height, counters, ascenders and descenders, thicks and thins, vertical stress)? What retinal variations of design occur? What is their significance (associative, selective, ordered)?
2. What is the basic point size of type? What retinal variations of size occur? What is their significance (selective, ordered, proportional)?
3. What is the basic style of type (i.e., bold, italic, underlined, outline, shadow, positive/negative images, chromatic/achromatic, upper/lower case)? What retinal variations of style occur? What is their significance (associative, selective, ordered, proportional)?
4. What is the basic horizontal and vertical spacing (i.e., line length, leading, alignment)? What retinal variations of spacing occur? What is their significance (associative, selective, ordered, proportional)?

Illustrations
Tables
1. What are the typographical characteristics of each table (i.e., design, size, style, and spacing)? What retinal variations of design, size, style, and spacing occur? What is their significance (associative, selective, ordered, proportional)?
2. What are the illustrative characteristics of each table (e.g., boxing, color, screens)? What retinal variations of the illustrative characteristics occur? What is the significance of the retinal variations (associative, selective, ordered, proportional)?

Figures
1. What are the illustrative characteristics of each figure (i.e., pictorial/non-pictorial)? What retinal variations of the illustrative characteristics occur? What is the significance of the retinal variations (associative, selective, ordered, proportional)?
2. What are the typographical characteristics of each figure (i.e., design, size, style, and spacing)? What retinal variations of design, size, style, and spacing occur? What is their significance (associative, selective, ordered, proportional)?
3. Do the illustrative and typographical characteristics of each figure communicate or reinforce a single and unified meaning?
4. Does each figure encourage viewing as opposed to reading? How is this achieved?

Page Design
1. What is the basic page grid? What retinal variations of this page grid occur (e.g., column number, column width, margin size)? What is the significance of the retinal variations (associative, selective, ordered, proportional)?
2. Which pages of the publication deserve the reader's initial attention? the reader's subsequent attention? Why? Do these pages solicit this attention? How?
3. Which illustrations on each page deserve the reader's initial attention? the reader's subsequent attention? Why? Do these illustrations solicit this attention? How?
4. Which blocks of typography on each page deserve the reader's initial attention? the reader's subsequent attention? Why? Do these blocks of typography solicit this attention? How?

Production
1. Does the printing process harmonize with the typography, illustrations, and page design?
2. Does the paper harmonize with the typography, illustrations, and page design?
3. Does the folding/binding process harmonize with the typography, illustrations, and page design?

Figure E.1. (Cont'd.)

Bibliography

Aristotle, *Rhetoric*, W. R. Roberts (trans.), The Modern Library, New York, 1954.

Barton, B. F., and M. S. Barton, Toward a Rhetoric of Visuals for the Computer Era, *The Technical Writing Teacher, 12*, pp. 126-145, 1985.

Benson, P. J., Writing Visually: Design Considerations in Technical Publications, *Technical Communication, 32*, pp. 35-39, 1985.

Bernhardt, S., Seeing the Text, *College Composition and Communication, 35*, pp. 66-78, 1986.

Bertin, J., *Graphics and Graphic Information-Processing*, W. J. Berg and P. Scott (trans.), Walter de Gruyter & Co., Berlin, 1981.

Bertin, J., *Semiology of Graphics*, W. J. Berg (trans.), University of Wisconsin Press, Madison, 1983.

Booher, H. R., Relative Comprehensibility of Pictorial Information and Printed Words in Procedural Instruction, *Human Factors, 17*, pp. 266-277, 1975.

Brandt, H. F., *The Psychology of Seeing*, Philosophical Library, New York, 1945.

Burke, K., The Five Key Terms of Dramatism, in *Contemporary Rhetoric*, W. R. Winterowd, (ed.), Harcourt Brace Jovanovich, New York, pp. 183-199, 1975.

Burnham, R. W., R. M. Hanes, and C. J. Bartleson, *Color: A Guide to Basic Facts and Concepts*, Wiley, New York, 1963.

Burt, C., *A Psychological Study of Typography*, Cambridge University Press, Cambridge, 1959.

Carosso, R., *Technical Communications*, Wadsworth, Belmont, CA, 1986.

Clark, H. H., and S. E. Haviland, Comprehension and the Given-New Contract, in *Discourse Production and Comprehension*, R. O. Freedle (ed.), Ablex, Norwood, NJ, pp. 1-40, 1977.

Clevinger, T., Jr., *Audience Analysis*, Bobbs-Merrill, Indianapolis, 1966.

Connors, R. J., *Actio*: A Rhetoric of Manuscripts, *Rhetoric Review, 2*, pp. 64-73, 1983.

Corbett, E. P. J., *Classical Rhetoric for the Modern Student*, 2nd edition, Oxford University Press, New York, 1971.

Craig, J., *Designing with Type*, rev. edition, Watson-Guptill, New York, 1980.

Crystal, D., and D. Davy, *Investigating English Style*, Indiana University Press, Bloomington, 1969.

DeVito, J. A., *The Psychology of Speech and Language*, Random House, New York, 1970.

Dowdey, D., Literary Science: A Rhetorical Analysis of an Essay Genre and Its Tradition, Diss. U. of Wisconsin, 1984.

Dwyer, F. M., *Strategies for Improving Visual Learning*, Learning Services, State College, PA, 1978.

Ede, L., and A. Lunsford, Audience Addressed/Audience Invoked: The Role of Audience in Composition Theory and Pedagogy, *College Composition and Communication, 35*, pp. 155-171, 1984.

Flower, L., *Problem-Solving Strategies for Writing*, 2nd edition, Harcourt Brace Jovanovich, New York, 1985.

Goldsmith, E., *Research into Illustration*, Cambridge University Press, Cambridge, 1984.

Halliday, M. A. K., and R. Hasan, *Cohesion in English*, Longman, London, 1976.

Hill, F. I., The Rhetoric of Aristotle, in A Synoptic History of Classical Rhetoric, J. J. Murphy (ed.), Hermagoras Press, Davis, California, pp. 19-76, 1983.

Kaufmann, G., *Visual Imagery and its Relation to Problem Solving*, Unversitetsforlaget, Bergen, Norway, 1979.

Kinneavy, J. L., *A Theory of Discourse*, Norton, New York, 1971.

Koran, M. L., and J. J. Koran, Interaction of Learner Characteristics with Pictorial Adjuncts in Learning from Science Text, *Journal of Research in Science Teaching*, 17, pp. 477-483, 1980.

Lanham, R. A., *Revising Business Prose*, Scribner's, New York, 1981.

Lauer, J. M., G. Montague, A. Lunsford, and J. Emig, *Four Worlds of Writing*, 2nd edition, Harper & Row, New York, 1985.

Lindemann, E., *A Rhetoric for Writing Teachers*, Oxford University Press, New York, 1982.

Mathes, J. C., and D. W. Stevenson, *Designing Technical Reports*, Bobbs-Merrill, Indianapolis, 1976.

Meador, P. A., Jr., Quintilian and the *Institutio oratoria*, in *A Synoptic History of Classical Rhetoric*, J. J. Murphy (ed.), Hermagoras Press, Davis, California, pp. 151-176, 1983.

Murch, G. M., Using Color Effectively: Designing to Human Specifications, *Technical Communication, 32*, pp. 14-20, 1985.

Ochs, D. J., Cicero's Rhetorical Theory, in *A Synoptic History of Classical Rhetoric*, J. J. Murphy (ed.), Hermagoras Press, Davis, California, pp. 90-150, 1983.

Ong, W. J., The Writer's Audience is Always a Fiction, *Publication of the Modern Language Association, 90*, pp. 9-21, 1975.

Paivio, A., *Imagery and Verbal Processes*, Holt, Rinehart, & Winston, New York, 1971.

Pitkin, W. L., Discourse Blocs, *College Composition and Communications, 20*, pp. 138-148, 1969.

Pitkin, W. L., Hierarchies and the Discourse of Hierarchy, *College English, 38*, pp. 648-659, 1977.

Quirk, R., et al., *A Grammar of Contemporary English*, Longman, London, 1972.

Rodgers, P. C., Jr., A Discourse-Centered Rhetoric of the Paragraph, *College Composition and Communication, 17*, pp. 2-11, 1966.

Rodgers, P. C., Jr., Alexander Bain and the Rise of the Organic Paragraph, *Quarterly Journal of Speech, 51*, pp. 399-408, 1965.

Rodgers, P. C., Jr., The Stadium of Discourse, *College Composition and Communication, 18*, pp. 178-185, 1967.

Salomon, G., Internalization of Filmic Schematic Operations in Interaction with Learners' Aptitudes, *Journal of Educational Psychology, 66*, pp. 499-511, 1974.

Sawyer, T. M., Why Speech Will Not Totally Replace Writing, *College Composition and Communication, 18*, pp. 43-48, 1977.

Shaughnessy, M., *Errors and Expectations*, Oxford University Press, New York, 1977.

Shearer, N. A., Alexander Bain and the Rise of the Organic Paragraph, *Quarterly Journal of Speech, 51*, pp. 399-408, 1965.

Sommers, N., Responding to Student Writing, *College Composition and Communication, 33*, pp. 148-156, 1982.

Tinker, M. A., *Legibility of Print*, Iowa State University Press, Ames, 1963.

Trim, J. L. M., Speech Education, in *The Teaching of English*, R. Quirk and A. H. Smith (eds.), Oxford University Press, London, pp. 60-86, 1964.

Woolbert, C. H., Speaking and Writing—A Study of Differences, *Quarterly Journal of Speech Education, 8*, pp. 271-285, 1922.

Zachrisson, B., *Studies in Legibility of Printed Text*, Almqvist & Wiskell, Stockholm, 1965.

Index

Contributors

SAM DRAGGA is Assistant Professor of English and Coordinator of the Writing Specialization (a writing-across-the-curriculum program) at Texas A&M University. His publications include articles on the evaluation and teaching of writing, interpretation of editorially problematic texts, and computer-based instruction. He has been the editor of a company newspaper and is currently the copy editor of a professional journal.

GWENDOLYN GONG is Associate Professor of English and Director of Freshman English Studies at Texas A&M University. She is the author of several articles on rhetorical theory, linguistics, and technical communication. She has taught writing internationally and has given numerous presentations at the national meetings of composition teachers and professional communicators.